Situation Comedy: Humor in Recent Art

Published to accompany the traveling exhibition, ***Situation Comedy: Humor in Recent Art***, organized and circulated by Independent Curators International (iCI), New York.

The exhibition is curated by Dominic Molon and Michael Rooks.

Exhibition Funders

The exhibition, tour, and catalogue are made possible, in part, by grants from the Elizabeth Firestone Graham Foundation and The Horace W. Goldsmith Foundation, with additional support from the iCI International Associates, the iCI Exhibition Partners, and the iCI independents.

Exhibition Itinerary *

The Contemporary Museum
Honolulu, Hawaii
September 9 - December 31, 2005

Chicago Cultural Center
Chicago, Illinois
February 4 – April 9, 2006

Winnipeg Art Gallery
Winnipeg, Manitoba, Canada
June 10 – September 10, 2006

Museum of Art/ Fort Lauderdale
Fort Lauderdale, Florida
June 1 – September 3, 2007

*at time of publication

Cover image: Martin Kersels, ***Tossing a Friend (Melinda) (1, 2, and 3)***, 1996 (detail, see p. 40)

Situation Comedy: Humor in Recent Art

Dominic Molon
and
Michael Rooks

Independent Curators International, New York

with an excerpt from ME TALK PRETTY ONE DAY by
David Sedaris

table of contents

foreword and acknowledgments 6
Judith Olch Richards

Comedy Is Not Pretty 8
Dominic Molon
and Michael Rooks

plates 10

The First Six Moments from Twelve Moments in the Life of the Artist 60
David Sedaris

exhibition checklist 66
lenders to the exhibition 70
iCI board of trustees 70

Christian Jankowski 10
Erika Rothenberg 13
Luis Gispert 14
Bob and Roberta Smith 17
Dave Muller 18
Olav Westphalen 19
David Shrigley 20
Michael Elmgreen and Ingar Dragset 23
Felix Gmelin 24
William Pope.L 26
Susan Smith-Pinelo 28
Cary Liebowitz 30
Michael Smith 32
Peter Land 33
Rodney Graham 34
Alexej Koschkarow 36
Tom Friedman 38
Martin Kersels 40
Tony Tasset 41
Dana Schutz 42
Lawrence Seward 45
Erwin Wurm 46
David Robbins 48
John Waters 51
Kelly Mark 52
Stephanie Brooks 53
Kay Rosen 54
Richard Prince 56
Laura Nova 58

foreword and acknowledgments

Artists throughout the ages have created works that use humor to convey ideas that can be understood best through the vocabulary of comedy. In recent years, during this period of widespread political upheaval, artists internationally have injected a healthy dose of humor, both light-hearted and dark, into their work, utilizing the leveling power of comedy—irony, slapstick and every other form—to break down barriers of taste, to question authority, and to encourage laughter in the museum environment, a place it is not often heard.

Exploring this development in artistic practice, *Situation Comedy* presents about sixty works—a selection of video and sound installations, paintings, sculptures, drawings, and photographs—by some thirty younger as well as more established artists working primarily in North America and Europe. The various forms of humor and range of mediums employed in this exhibition result in a visually, intellectually, and emotionally stimulating presentation, one that presents viewers with a thought-provoking source of laughs, smiles, smirks, groans, and giggles. It engenders a sense of immediacy and familiarity, while simultaneously working as a means of critical engagement, rather than simply as entertainment.

This catalogue and traveling exhibition have been made possible through the encouragement, dedication, and generosity of a great many people. First and foremost, on behalf of iCI's Board of Trustees and staff, I extend our sincere thanks and appreciation to the distinguished curators of the exhibition, Dominic Molon, Pamela Alper Associate Curator at the Museum of Contemporary Art, Chicago, and Michael Rooks, curator at The Contemporary Museum, Honolulu, with whom it has been a pleasure to work. With intelligence, wit, and persistence, they have presented a compelling and timely subject through their selection of a rich and provocative range of works, and have composed a text that gives us not only a better understanding of the objects on view, but also a sense of why humor of all kinds is to be found at the center of contemporary art practice.

We are delighted to have the opportunity to include in this book an excerpt from the essay, "Twelve Moments in the Life of the Artist," from *ME TALK PRETTY ONE DAY*, by David Sedaris, and I take this opportunity to express our warmest appreciation to him for his kind permission to do so. This wickedly funny tale of his days as an art student is a perfect complement to the exhibition. Our sincere thanks go to those who helped make this possible, including Amanda S. Guccione, Subsidiary Rights Associate, Little, Brown and Company (Inc.), and Susan Sayre Batton.

The curators join me in expressing our gratitude to all the artists in this exhibition, and to voice our special appreciation to Luis Gispert, Laura Nova, David Robbins, Michael

Smith, John Waters, and Erwin Wurm for their extra efforts. We are also indebted to the lenders who have generously allowed their works to travel throughout the two-year tour, and to colleagues at museums and galleries who assisted throughout the curatorial process, including, in particular, Christine Burgin, Christine Burgin Gallery, New York; Rene de Guzman, visual arts curator, Yerba Buena Center for the Arts, San Francisco; Matthew Distel, associate curator, Contemporary Art Center, Cincinnati; Zach Feuer, Zach Feuer Gallery (LFL), New York; Alexandra Frank, Erwin Wurm's studio; Hudson, Feature Inc., New York; Kevin Hull, Fusebox, Washington, D.C.; Christine Kim, associate curator, Studio Museum in Harlem; Jay Sanders, Marianne Boesky Gallery, New York; and Elizabeth A.T. Smith, James W. Alsdorf Chief Curator, and Francesco Bonami, Manilow Senior Curator, Museum of Contemporary Art, Chicago.

The production of this exhibition catalogue is funded, in part, by a grant from the Elizabeth Firestone Graham Foundation, and I want to underscore the vital importance of that generous support, for which we are most grateful. Also crucial to the development of this exhibition are funds from The Horace W. Goldsmith Foundation, and additional support from the iCI International Associates and the iCI independents.

Special thanks from the curators and iCI to Georgianna Lagoria, director, The Contemporary Museum, Honolulu, where the exhibition premieres, and to Robert Fitzpatrick, director and CEO, the Museum of Contemporary Art, Chicago, for the enthusiastic support they have both shown for this project. iCI is grateful to Gregory Knight, director of the Chicago Cultural Center, one of the presenters of *Situation Comedy*, for his generous assistance, and thanks go to all of the institutions that will present this exhibition as it travels; it is through their efforts that the project has become a reality.

Sincere appreciation is due to mgmt., especially to Ariel Apte and Rachel Griffin, for their graphic design of this book, and to Deborah Drier, the book's editor. It was a great pleasure to work with these superb professionals.

iCI's dedicated, knowledgeable, and enthusiastic staff deserves recognition for their work on every aspect of this project, from securing loans and images, developing the tour, arranging for the packing and shipping, to creating this publication. Thanks for this work go especially to Susan Hapgood, director of exhibitions; Beverly Parsons, registrar; and Melissa Pomerantz, exhibitions assistant. Thanks also to Amy Owen, exhibitions associate and publications coordinator; and Sue Scott, executive assistant and press coordinator, as well as to former exhibitions intern Margaret Martin. I also want to express my gratitude to Hedy Roma, director of development, and to development assistants Hilary Fry and Katie Holden for their successful fund-raising efforts.

Finally, I extend my warmest appreciation to iCI's Board of Trustees for their steadfast support, enthusiasm, and commitment to all of iCI's activities. They join me in expressing our gratitude to everyone who has contributed to making possible this challenging and gratifying project.

Judith Olch Richards
Executive Director

Comedy Is Not Pretty

Dominic Molon
and Michael Rooks

Much of the rhetoric about what constitutes important contemporary art has been defined in major thematic group exhibitions that take up such human concerns as social justice, economic inequity, healthcare issues, political hegemony, and the environment. As a result, grimly earnest assessments of the vicissitudes of geopolitics have become the defining expressions of the moment and are presented with the insistent sense of authority that such matters demand, crowding out opportunities to address them with levity and a sense of the absurd. The emphasis on art as a form of education or as an agent for social change is particularly at odds with work that encourages laughter, perhaps because its imperatives fail to recognize the redemption that humor can offer from recognition that we are complicit in the misfortunes and inequities of contemporary reality. Art in the service of social change tends to frame a subject in the documentary tradition, presenting a subjective point of view in order to achieve an objective consensus on the nature of given truths: an acknowledgment of the world that offers reconciliation between the viewer and the subject of the artist's critique by offering largely accepted and sympathetic viewpoints. In other words, it tends to preach to the choir, submitting binaries that are passively accepted more often than not. Humor, on the other hand, makes us responsible for our foolishness, greed, hatred, and other shortcomings by making the object of its mockery personal and familiar. Humor exposes the individual and collective horror and regret that our personal failings cause, and laughter provides a cathartic release from them, though it can also be unforgiving. Through a process of self-indictment, trial, and absolution, humor gives us the opportunity to make amends with ourselves and the world through the recognition of the guilt and pathos we share with others, and it reveals how out of step our behavior may be in relation to changing social standards. In doing so, it can be hostile, aggressive, and confrontational. This antagonistic aspect of humor can be traced back to writers such as Charles Baudelaire who once noted that laughter requires a "Satanic" evocation of feelings of superiority,[1] while the British journalist and literary critic Arthur Koestler observed that nearly all modern theories of laughter recognize "a component of malice, of debasement of the other fellow, and of aggressive-defensive self-assertion."[2] In the rarified milieu of contemporary art, where euphemistic terms are coined and perennially reminted, in order to avoid offense and redress unconscious social biases, the present challenge of incorporating humor into the aesthetic situation recalls comedian Steve Martin's assertion after a particularly chauvinistic gag, "Hey ... wait a second ... comedy is *not* pretty!"[3]

Situation Comedy is intended as a reminder of the strong presence of the comedic gesture in contemporary art. It emphasizes the comedic as both a necessary foil and complement to prevailing curatorial tendencies, encouraging laughter alongside contrition and emphasizing the transformative potential of humor in contrast to the stifling effect of dogma. The exhibition presents art from the past fifteen years (with an emphasis on more recent works) by an international group of artists working in painting, sculpture, installation, sound, photography, and video. The works in the exhibition range from video and photographs documenting staged pratfalls and sight gags, to text-based works that playfully subvert aspects of language itself or present absurdly pathetic comments and observations. This essay examines the numerous comedic subcategories engaged by contemporary artists, including slapstick, self-effacing humor, art-related satire, failure and/or the pathetic, text inversion and word play, jokes, physical exaggeration, and the broader notion of "situational comedy" from which the exhibition takes its name. It also recognizes contemporary artists' incorporation of humorous strategies and effects as a form of critical engagement rather than as a gesture towards entertainment, while simultaneously recognizing the ability of the comedic to give the viewer a sense of immediacy and familiarity.

The Double Take

One of the most significant ways that artists have manifested elements of the humorous in their work has been through a process of *détournement*—a concept developed by the radical Situationists of the 1950s and 1960s, in which the preexisting structures and procedures of daily life are calculatedly subverted.[4] In the process, the mundane becomes comically estranged and fantastic, prompting the viewer to recognize much of the absurdity that characterizes his or her daily life. For example, Christian Jankowski's video documentation of his 1992 performance, *The Hunt*, takes that quintessential quotidian event of supermarket shopping and elevates it to mock-epic proportions. The means of acquiring sustenance for oneself or one's family in the modern age—purchasing pre-packaged goods in an antiseptic man-made environment—is contrasted with the action that defined this activity in a more primitive time—hunting live animals with a bow and arrow. Jankowski's intentional introduction of a needless degree of skill and difficulty into such an everyday occupation, and his ridiculous transformation of an innocuous domestic chore into a hypermasculine rite, creates a discomforting recognition of the extent to which our lives have become divorced from active engagement with the world around us. His video *Flock*, 2002,

Christian Jankowski

***The Hunt*, 1992**
Single-channel video with sound
1 minute, 11 seconds
Collection of the artist;
courtesy maccarone, inc., New York
and Klosterfelde, Berlin

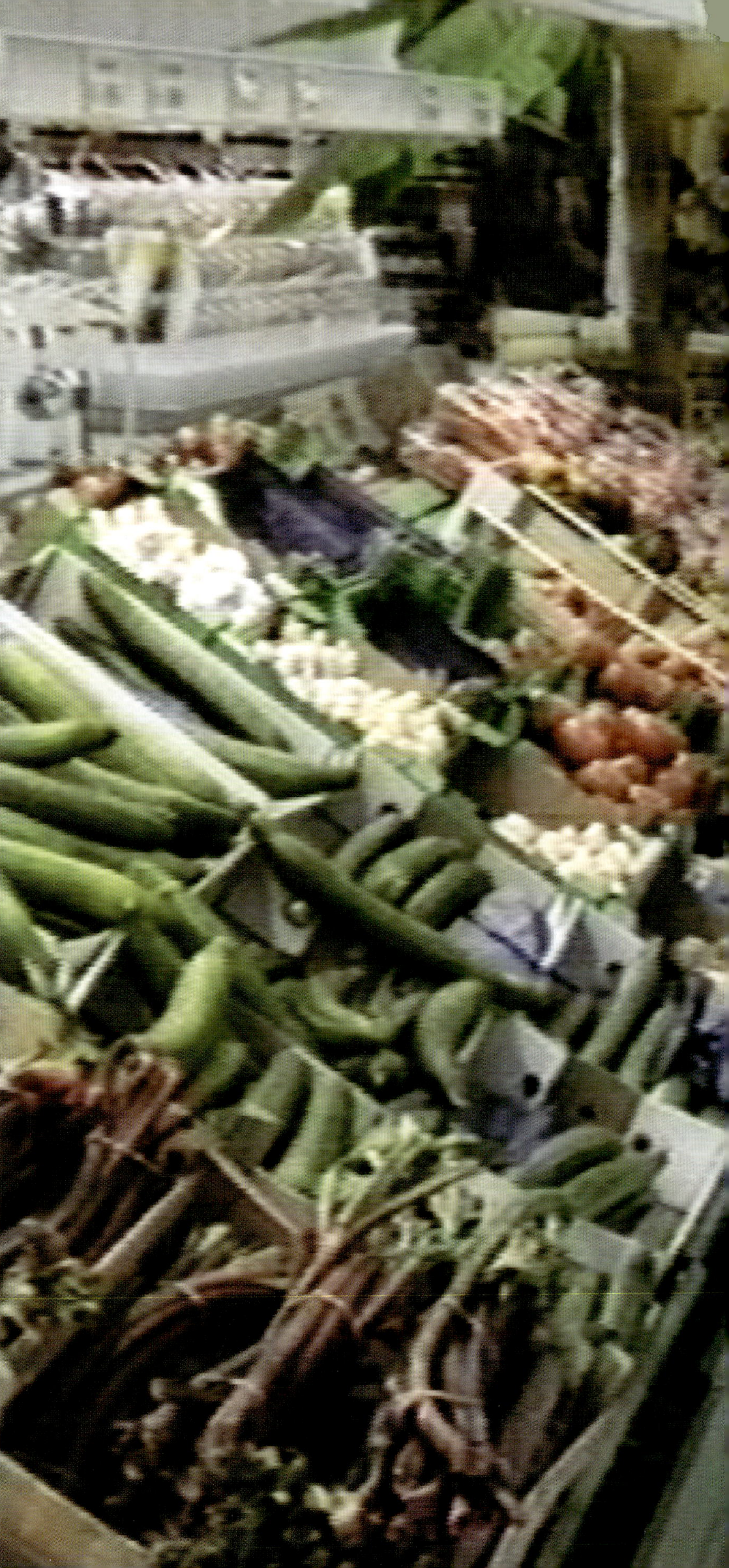

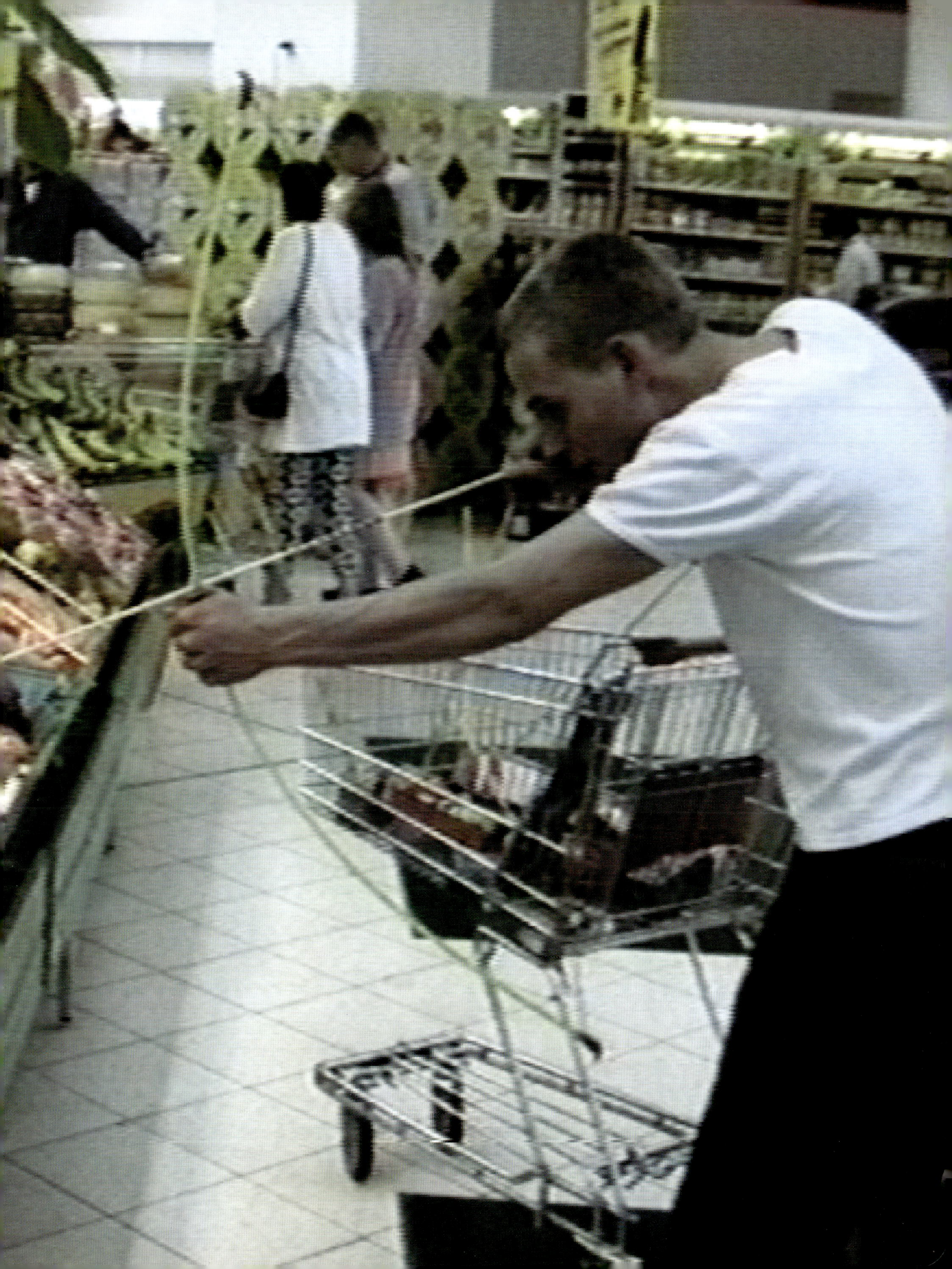

deals with the less pedestrian, yet still common occasion of an art gallery opening. The transformative potential of art viewing is made literal by a magician who changes gallery-goers into sheep. The absurdity of the bleating flock as it tours the exhibition recalls the opening scene of Jacques Tati's 1954 masterpiece, *M. Hulot's Holiday*, in which a group of tourists patiently await a train's arrival. Confused by incomprehensible announcements over the public address system, they move en masse from one platform to the next, always missing their train. As in Tati's film, moving from one place to the next—in the case of *Flock* to a higher level of awareness—is frustrated by the group's willingness to trust the magician's contrivance. They thus surrender confidence in the potential agency of transport that art can offer, for as herd animals they no longer possess conscious agency. At the same time, Jankowski sardonically comments on the herd mentality of the contemporary art world's upper echelons.

Erika Rothenberg's *Another Century of Progress*, 1999-2000, similarly redirects our expectations of a familiar emblem of the contemporary social sphere, here, a sign typically found in American town halls, community centers, and churches. The list of the week's activities comprises, unsurprisingly, various kinds of "group therapy" such as "Alcoholics Anonymous" or altruistic programs like a soup kitchen for the poor. Stranger events of the week, such as "Parenting Your Clone" and "Singles Support Group: Finding Love on Other Planets" become apparent upon further consideration, comically rationalized by the date of the sign—January 4, 2100. Rothenberg's sarcastic conjecture that human nature will change very little in a century is further underscored by the title of Sunday's sermon (and the work itself): "Another Century of Progress."

A less positive element of our daily experience, the annoying and often seemingly interminable noise of a car alarm receives a hilarious reinterpretation in Luis Gispert's video *Block Watching*, 2002–03. In this work, an attractive young blond woman dressed as a cheerleader (yet incongruously adorned with gaudy gold jewelry more in keeping with the "bling bling" posturing of hip-hop) lip-synchs the sound of a typical car alarm. The resulting performance is an unusual translation of technological sounds into human gestures and extreme facial expressions, the latter evoking Henri Bergson's idea that "a face is all the more comic the more nearly it suggests to us the idea of some simple mechanical action in which its personality would forever be absorbed."[5] The young woman mocks the alarm in a childishly obstinate game usually aimed at frustrating authority, spoofing gangsta rap's blustery, antagonistic patter and reducing its adult-themed content to child's play. At the same time, *Block Watching* relates hysterically to the general annoyance of car alarms as they impotently blare their warnings to an indifferent public. Gispert's conflation of the practiced aggression of street culture and the dispassionate aggression of the street-based car alarm with the simultaneously innocent/eroticized figure of the cheerleader enhances the work's comedic affect.

Erika Rothenberg

***Another Century of Progress*, 1999–2000**
Aluminum and acrylic signboard, plastic letters
36 x 24 x 1¾ inches (91.4 x 61 x 4.4 cm)
Collection of the artist; courtesy Zolla/Lieberman Gallery, Chicago

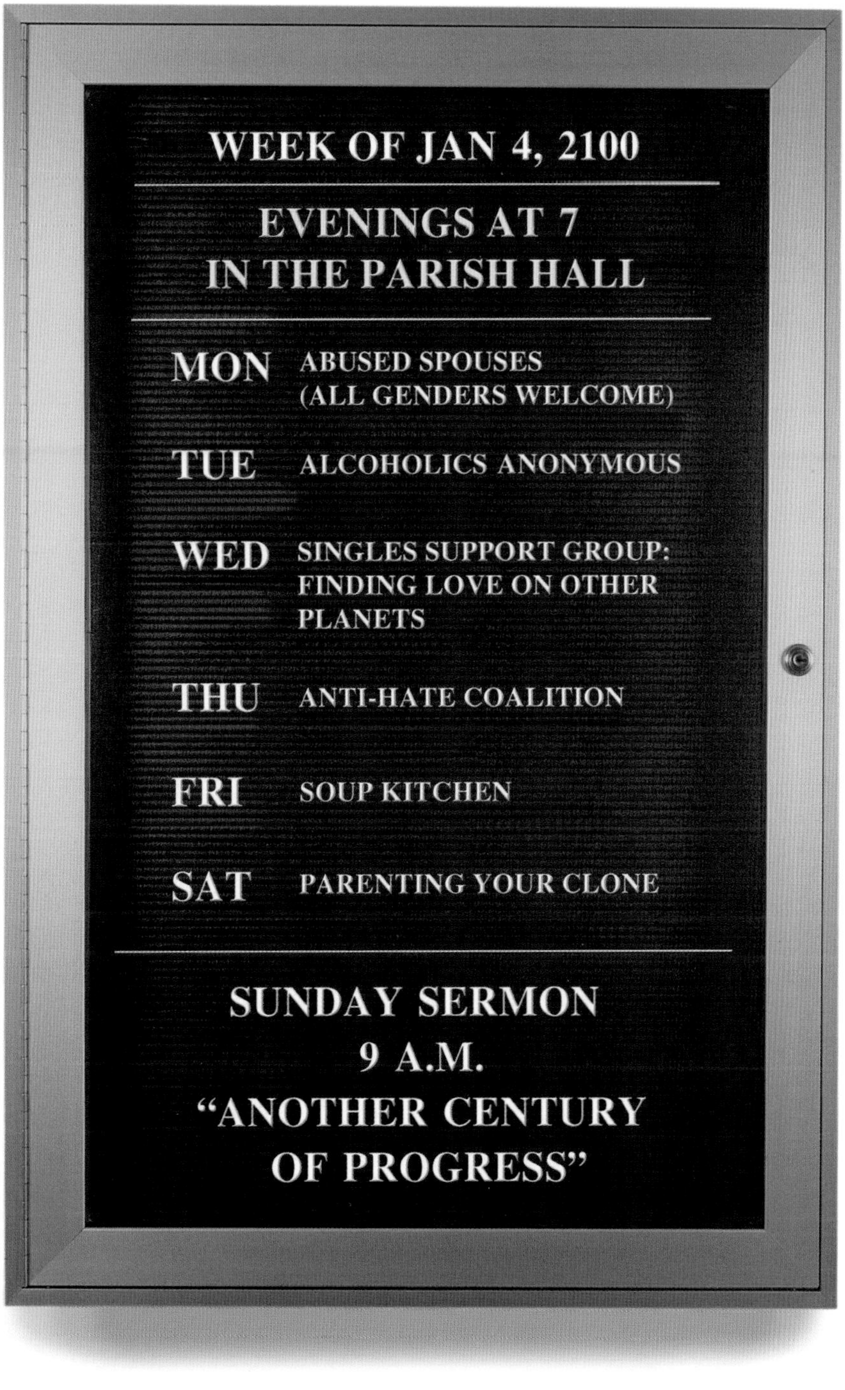

WEEK OF JAN 4, 2100

EVENINGS AT 7
IN THE PARISH HALL

MON ABUSED SPOUSES
(ALL GENDERS WELCOME)

TUE ALCOHOLICS ANONYMOUS

WED SINGLES SUPPORT GROUP:
FINDING LOVE ON OTHER
PLANETS

THU ANTI-HATE COALITION

FRI SOUP KITCHEN

SAT PARENTING YOUR CLONE

SUNDAY SERMON
9 A.M.
"ANOTHER CENTURY
OF PROGRESS"

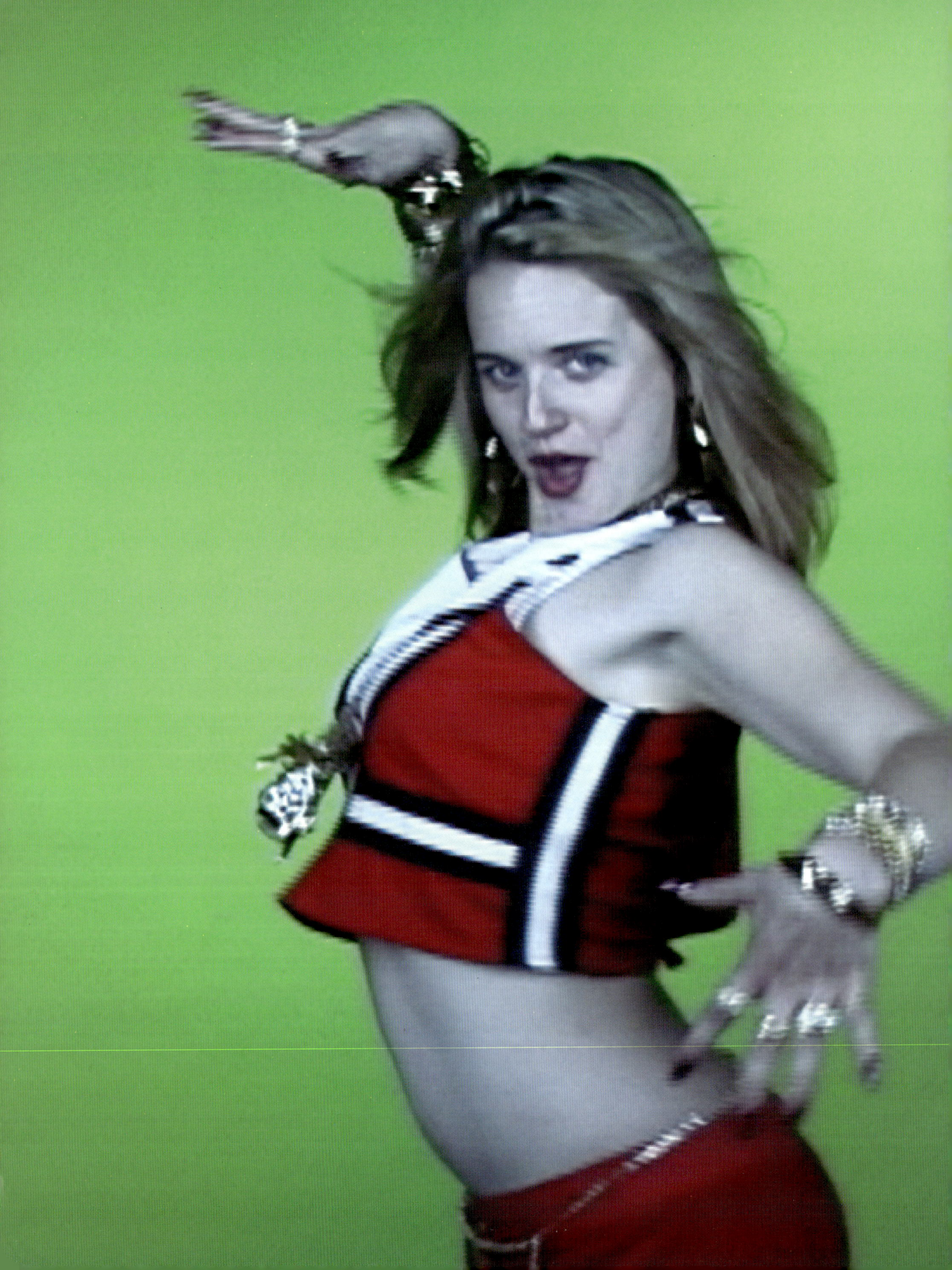

Luis Gispert

Block Watching, 2002–03
Single-channel video with sound
1 minute, 57 seconds
Collection of the artist;
courtesy Zach Feuer Gallery (LFL), New York

Art in the Satirical Crosshairs [or Satire Aimed at Art]

Much of the work in *Situation Comedy* is not unsurprisingly engaged with satirizing the seriousness of high art culture itself. The most irreverent example, perhaps, is found in the work of British artist Bob and Roberta Smith (aka Patrick Brill). Their/his very enterprise, a single artist assuming the identity of a male/female partnership, is evocative of comedy routines from the vaudeville tradition of "double-voiced vocalists" to Steve Martin and Lily Tomlin's combined role in the 1984 film *All of Me*. As the performer struggles with the competing interests and nature of its other half, a travesty of the Freudian conflict between the superego and the id ensues. In the case of Bob and Roberta Smith, the dual role that represses individual artistic identity sets up potentially comic confusion regarding authorship. Two works in the exhibition reflect the split art world personality that the pseudonym suggests. In their text banner proclaiming that "Artists Ruin it for Everyone," the Smiths perpetrate a knowing comment on artists' often self-proclaimed critical position towards the art establishment, visual culture, and society. Another banner conversely implores the viewer to "Make Your Own Damn Art," a mocking intimation of the artist's rejection of his duties of expression. Less bawdy and more conceptually cunning is Dave Muller's *He Could Sell Ice To...*, 2000, a reworking of an announcement for Gagosian Gallery's exhibition of Andy Warhol's notorious *Oxidation Paintings* of 1978, which were created through the act of Warhol and others urinating onto chemically prepared canvas. Here, an image of comic-strip character Calvin (from *Calvin and Hobbes*) naughtily peeing into space (an image often seen on pick-up truck windows as an assertion of a "bad boy" mentality) is grafted improbably into the high art space of the gallery announcement. Both a reflection of trends in current popular culture and an irreverent taunt aimed at the venerated reputation of so-called "blue-chip" art, the work simultaneously operates within Warhol's Pop art spirit while conflating absolutely incongruent white trash and elitist art world cultures.

A suite of works on paper by the German artist Olav Westphalen feature clever plays on cultural situations and glib phrases such as one depicting a frumpy tourist wearing wooden clogs, each respectively bearing the slogan "I ♥ Holland" and "I ♥ it Too." *Snowman*, 2002-03, is a send-up of academic exchanges typical in the art world where stock-in-trade phrases may sometimes describe abstract or theoretical ideas. The drawing reveals an absurd situation in which two snowmen engaged in sexual intercourse are discussing "reification," a word used to denote when an abstraction is described in terms that make it concrete and tangible. Asked by the dominant snowman "what's wrong with reification?," the passive snowman responds with the question "the word or the concept?," setting up a circular argument that underscores the nature of the term since the word "reification" made manifest in ink is itself an illustration of the concept, while the circular reasoning is suggested by the physical arrangement of the snowmens' linked bodies. In *Banana Peel*, 2002–03, the artist provides the classic setup for a pratfall in a simple rendering of a banana's empty skin

Bob and Roberta Smith
***Make Your Own Damn Art*, 2001**
Acrylic on cotton
73 x 70 inches (185.4 x 177.8 cm)
Collection of the artist;
courtesy Pierogi Gallery,
Brooklyn, New York

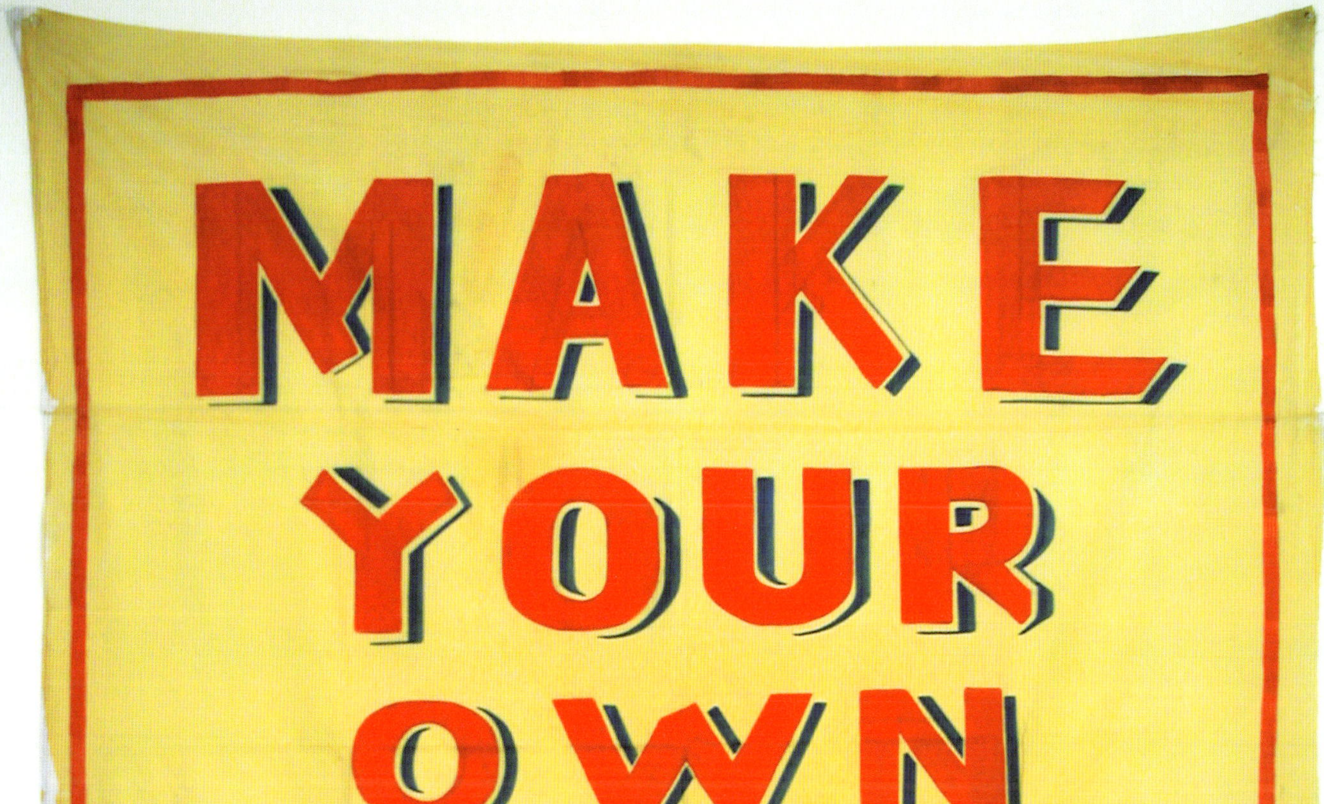

MAKE
YOUR
OWN
DAMN
ART

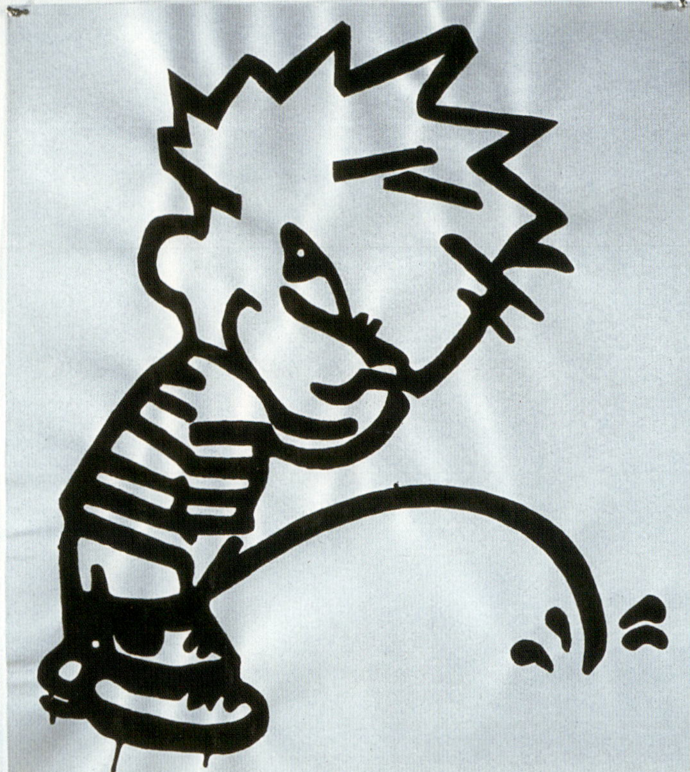

Dave Muller

He could sell ice to..., 2000
Acrylic and aluminum paint on paper
Two parts, 20 x 64 inches overall
(50.8 x 162.6 cm)
Private collection, New York

Olav Westphalen

Snowman, 2002–03
Acrylic and ink on paper
30 x 23 inches framed (76.2 x 58.4 cm)
Collection of the artist;
courtesy maccarone, inc., New York

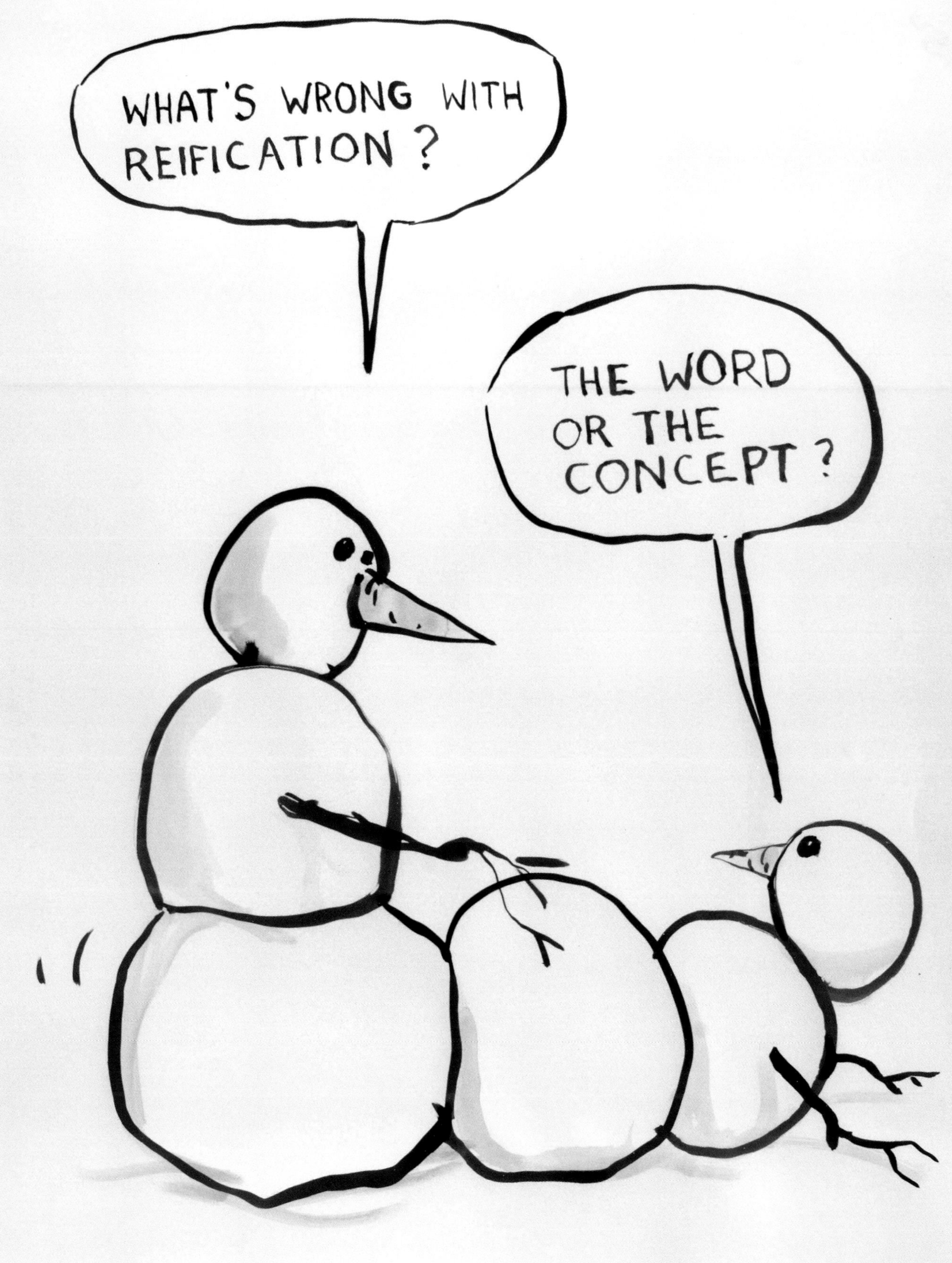
WHAT'S WRONG WITH REIFICATION?
THE WORD OR THE CONCEPT?

David Shrigley

Untitled (Notice), 1998
Chromogenic print
9 7/8 x 9 7/8 inches (25 x 25 cm)
Collection of Richard Lappin,
Brooklyn, New York

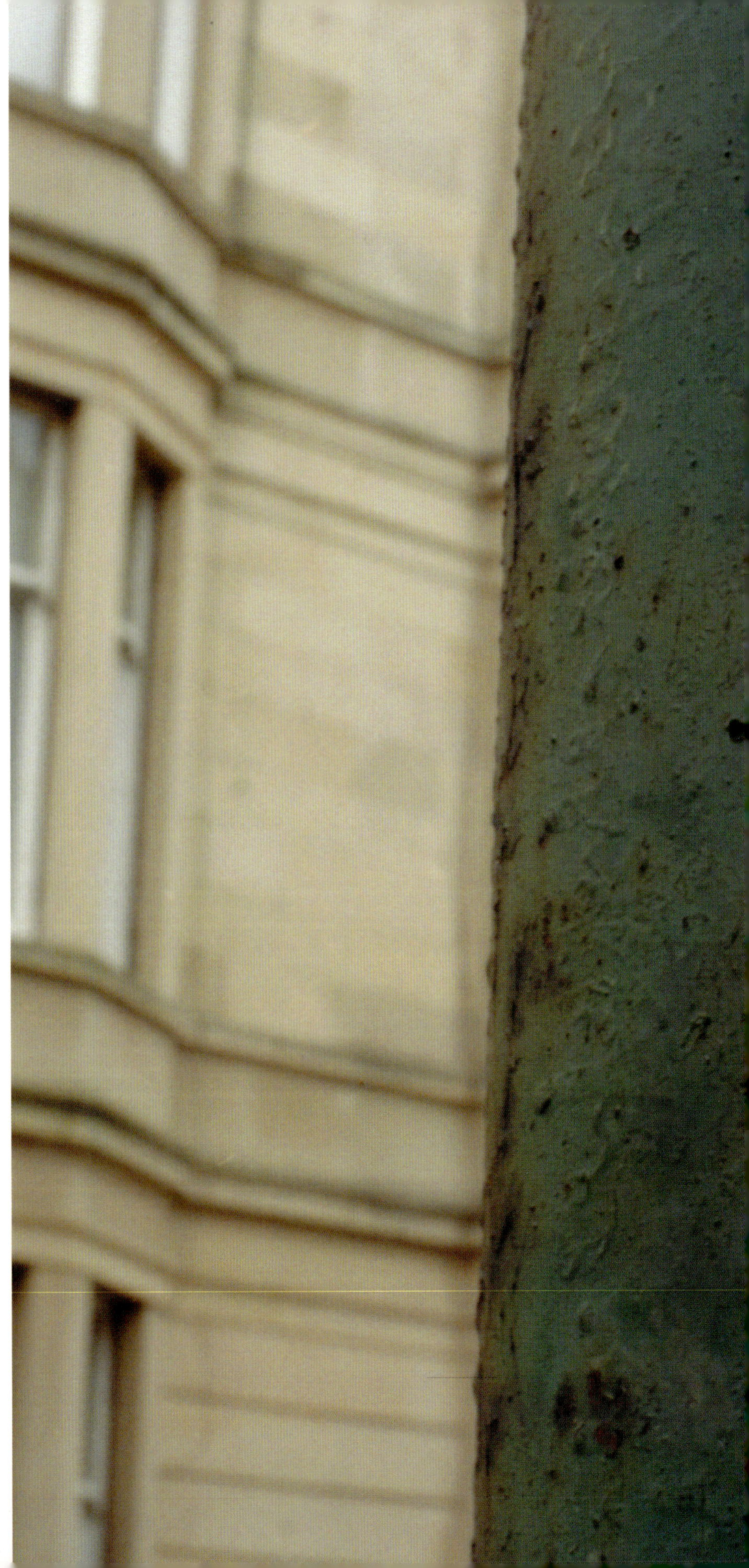

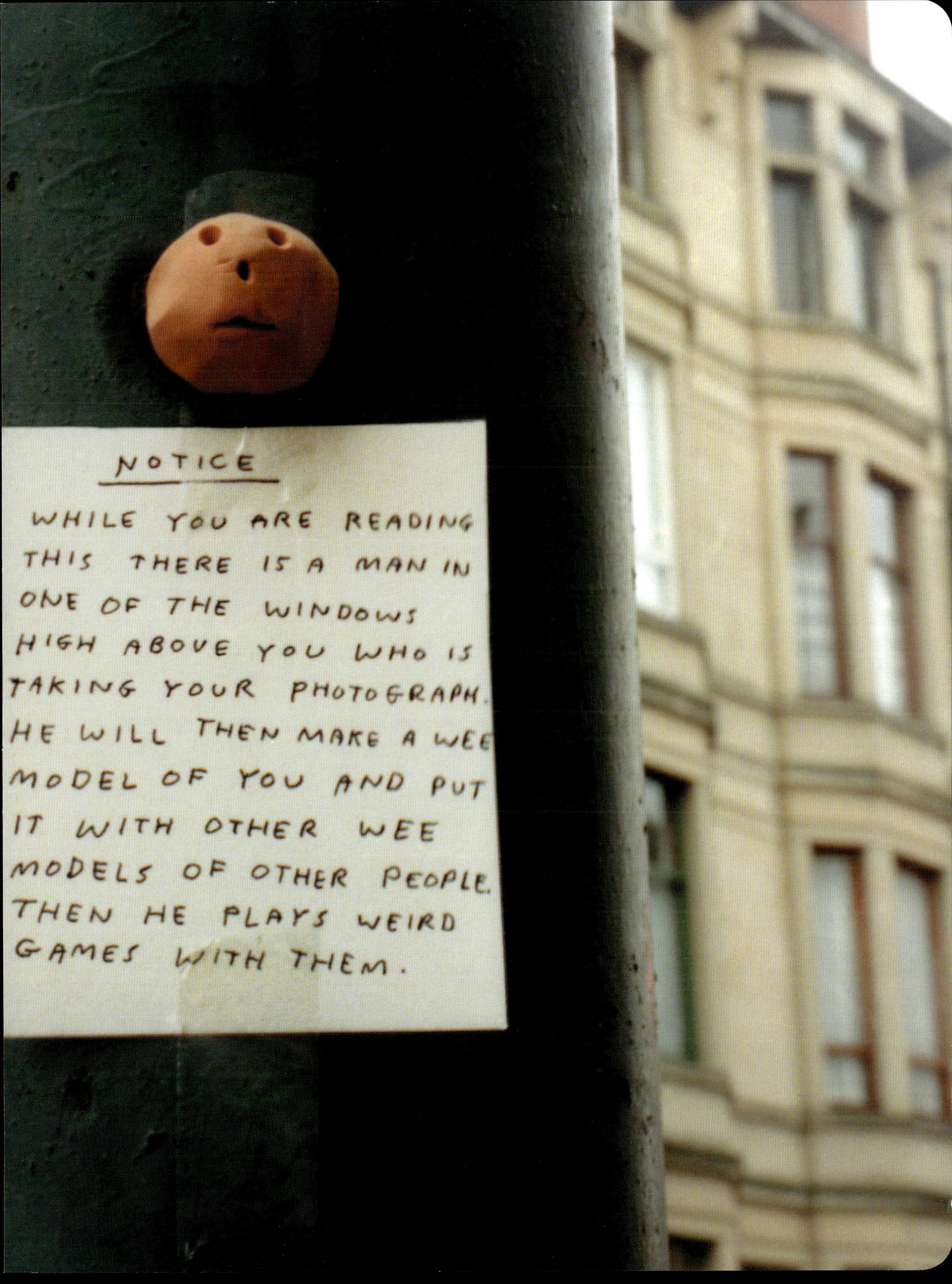
NOTICE
WHILE YOU ARE READING THIS THERE IS A MAN IN ONE OF THE WINDOWS HIGH ABOVE YOU WHO IS TAKING YOUR PHOTOGRAPH. HE WILL THEN MAKE A WEE MODEL OF YOU AND PUT IT WITH OTHER WEE MODELS OF OTHER PEOPLE. THEN HE PLAYS WEIRD GAMES WITH THEM.

lying on the ground, encouraging our expectation of the inevitable result while questioning conventional expectations of art's function and meaning. Such works possess the graphic style and comedic logic of *New Yorker* cartoons yet depart ever so slightly from these more popular representations by being either more oriented towards art-world/intellectual satire or more oblique in their humorous intent.

Like Westphalen, British artist David Shrigley is best known for his humorous drawings. However, rather than cartoonish, Shrigley's drawings are purposefully clumsy, resembling the work of an untrained artist or a child, with scrupulously ham-fisted text standing alone or printed alongside the images. His text often provides inane observations and absurdly pedestrian pronouncements such as "I build scaffolding and I know what I'm doing," or the stream-of-conscious succession of vows that follow the statement, "from now on I will do exactly as I am told." Recalling the work of the legendary American author and humorist, James Thurber, who contributed cartoons to *The New Yorker* for thirty-four years, Shrigley's drawings are inspired by unspoken thoughts, judgments, reckonings, and revelations derived from common experiences and thus manifest blunt, internalized representations of the world. As Thurber once said, "The humorist makes fun of himself, but in so doing, he identifies himself with people—that is, people everywhere, not for the purpose of taking them apart, but simply revealing their true nature."[6] Shrigley's slightly misanthropic take on human nature is transferred to the social realm in photographs that document public interventions and practical jokes. In *Drink Me*, 1998, a clear bottle filled with yellow liquid is left abandoned near a debris-strewn area of a tenement building, illustrating a juvenile urine-related prank. Another photograph, *Notice*, 1996, shows a hand-written sign that Shrigley has posted on a lamppost warning its reader that he or she is being observed by a weirdo with Play-Doh and a camera. These serve as reminders of the sort of anonymous and feeble acts of aggression one encounters unexpectedly in public, evoking amusement at the comedic gesture and embarrassment from playing the fool, while revealing the vulnerability of human nature.

Danish artists Michael Elmgreen and Ingar Dragset stage a private act of aggression in *Powerless Structures (Safe)*, 2000. Creating a situation that would be anything but laughable except for its conceit made obvious by the art gallery or museum context in which we encounter it, the work plays on the tendency of the wealthy to conceal one bit of wealth—valuable items in a safe—behind another—a painting—in this instance, a replica of a Robert Ryman painting. The artists utilize fundamental aspects of comedic misunderstanding and inversion: the thief doesn't understand the value of the artwork hanging in plain view and slashes it to get to the safe, while the collector neglects and disrespects the work's artistic value (while risking its market value) by using the painting itself to cloak "valuables." The work raises questions concerning moral and economic values, class and social status, and modern and Postmodern art ideas, in their relation to the art market. Such critical dynamics are illustrated by both the subjects (thief

Michael Elmgreen and Ingar Dragset

Powerless Structures (Safe), **2000**
Stainless steel, combination lock, canvas, and stretcher
35½ x 35½ x 2 inches
(90.2 x 90.2 x 5.1 cm)
Collection of Burt Minkoff, Lake Worth, Florida

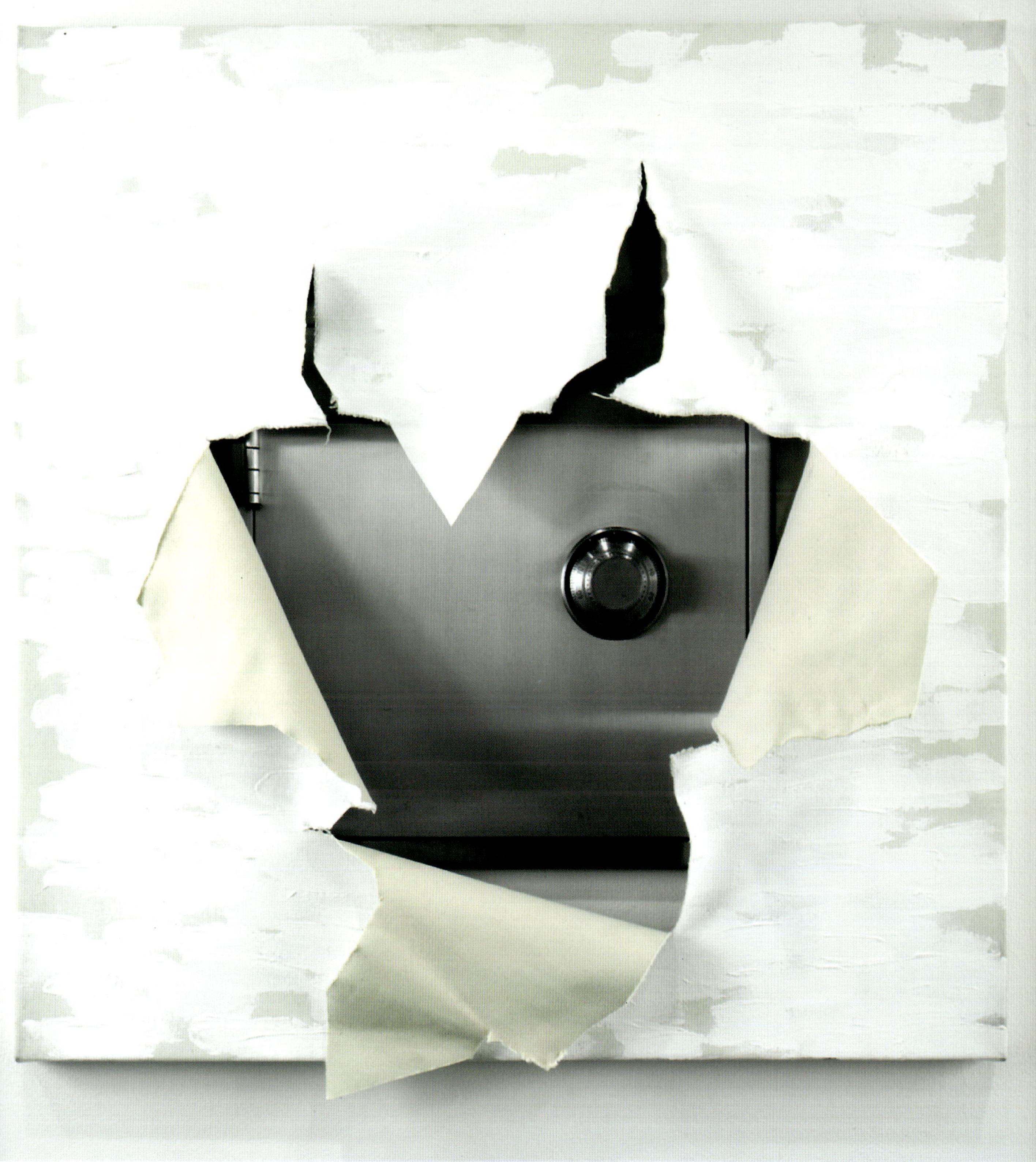

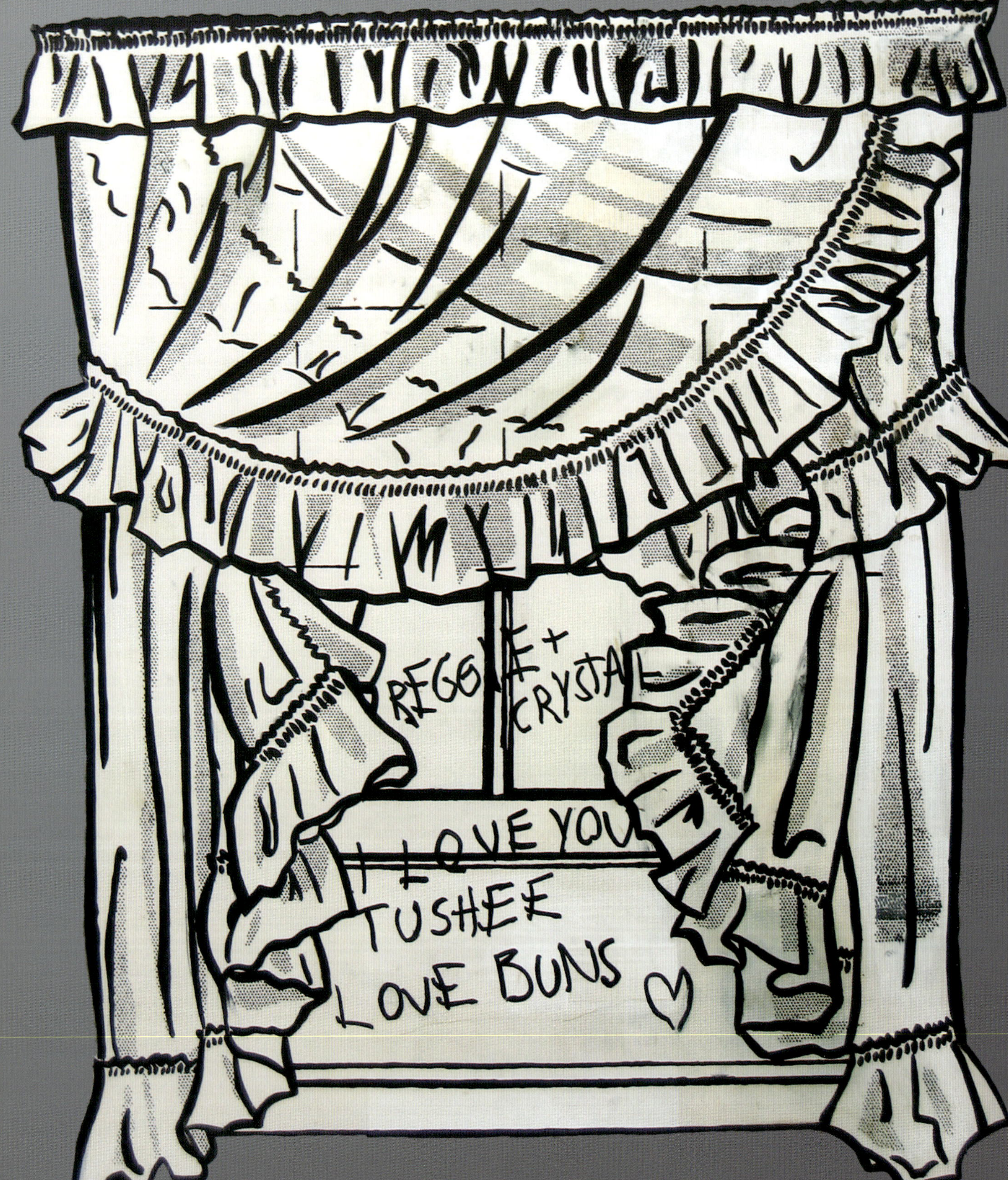
REGGIE +
CRYSTAL
I LOVE YOU
TUSHEE
LOVE BUNS

and collector) and objects (slash and concealment) of the work. They also come into play through an ability to decipher the hoax that is predicated on insider knowledge of the value of the Ryman, as well as the farce played out in the work between Ryman's structural fixation with painting, Lucio Fontana's transgressions against the canvas, and the conceptual nature of Elmgreen and Dragset's construct, which trumps them both.

I Love You Tushee Love Buns, 1994, by the Swedish artist Felix Gmelin, recreates an actual instance of vandalism to Pop art icon Roy Lichtenstein's painting *Curtain*, 1962, by a temporary guard at the Whitney Museum of American Art. In an anti-art gesture made under the pretense of adhering to the tenets of the American Pop movement, the guard jotted a tender note to his lover on the painting. Such an embarrassing public display of affection at the expense of the artist and the owner of the work is amplified by the resonance between the sophomoric act and the kitchy, ruffled curtains, while the absurdly sentimental nature of the graffiti lessens, to some degree, the seriousness of the defacing of an important work of art—a situation recognized by Gmelin with an exacting sense of irony.

Self-Effacing Humor

Redirecting wit's crosshairs to take aim at oneself, several artists in the exhibition strategically impose the unnerving state of self-humiliation to scrutinize issues of identity and to challenge the parochial notions that frame such issues in cultural theory. William Pope.L is best known for his performative work, in which humor is employed to lure his audience into a more serious consideration of the cultural conventions that perpetuate racism and its codified language (which functions in a way not dissimilar to the manner in which physical humor triggers intuitive responses to sets and subsets of meaning). *Foraging #1, #2*, and *#3*, 1995–98, are based on Pope.L's performative works titled *Black Domestic*, 1993–95, in which the artist dragged a plastic dairy cow around Manhattan on a leash while performing various acts, punctuating the performance with the question, "If a black person owns a cow, does the meaning of the cow change?" The black-and-white of the plastic Holstein, the whiteness of cow's milk, and the blackness of the artist's body provide the visual dynamics of Pope.L's performance, while the accompanying photographs depict the artist in varying degrees of self-effacement: suffocating in a cheap white plastic bag, grazing on hay like a farm animal, and (un)dressed as a pensive, toilet-brush-wielding bunny. Pope.L employs self-effacing humor to question the cultural meanings constructed around whiteness and blackness, emphasizing the inherent dualities and ambiguities that are overlooked in the binary representation of race.

Susan Smith-Pinelo emphasizes the human body in a quite different and more sexually specific way in her video *Sometimes*, 2001. Comprising a tightly cropped image of the artist heaving her bosom to the 1979 Michael

Felix Gmelin
***I Love You Tushee Love Buns (After Roy Lichtenstein [1962] and Reginald Walker [1993])*, 1994**
Oil on polyester
39 x 33½ inches framed (100 x 85 cm)
Collection of the artist;
courtesy Milliken, Stockholm, and maccarone, inc., New York

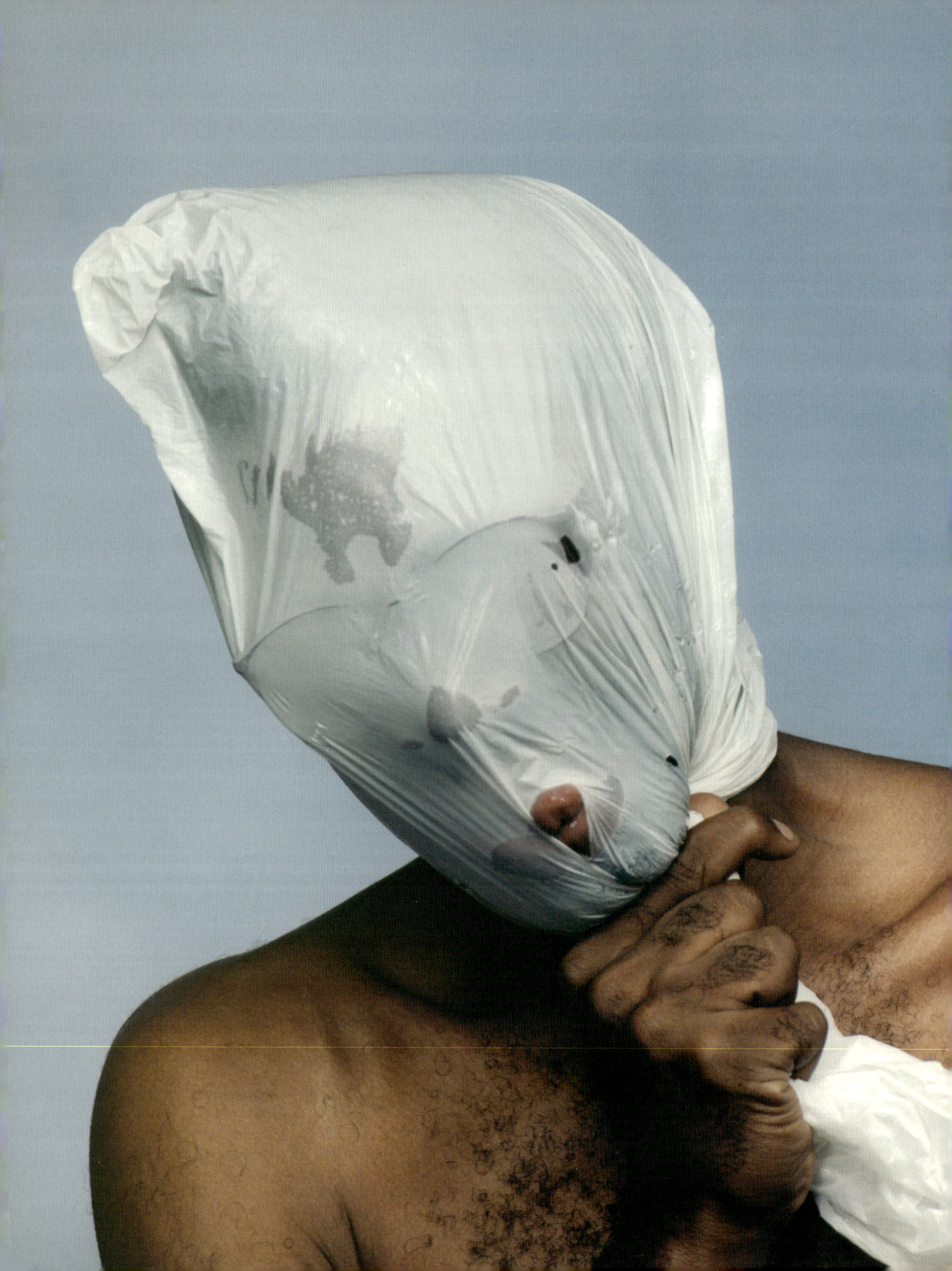

Jackson song "Working Day and Night," the work functions as a satire on the sexual objectification of black women in music videos (particularly rap and hip-hop). Smith-Pinelo underscores her point, perhaps, by wearing a necklace with a jeweled pendant reading "ghetto," critiquing the fixation on the female form by associating it with a "ghetto mentality." Like Pope.L, who obliquely addresses the racist stereotype of exaggerated sexual drive in black men, Smith-Pinelo tackles the objectification of black women by men of all stripes by "owning" and controlling it, while at the same time questioning the perpetuation of such representations by black artists in the entertainment industry.

Schlemiels, Losers, Stumblebums, and Nincompoops

Cary Liebowitz has dedicated much of his work to examining both the humble and the humiliating notions of selfhood. Recent paintings such as *Self Esteem 100 Dollars, Reduced to 5 Cents*, 1995, and *Please Check One*, 1999, take the demoralizations of everyday life and represent them through plaintive comments printed in a sad and almost child-like fashion. In *Self Esteem*, we are presented with a metaphor for the rapidly dwindling value of the artist's presumable sense of self-worth in a "for sale" sign listing former prices for self-esteem that have been slashed and incrementally replaced by lower ones. His 1999 installation of household trash bins emblazoned with the words "Gain!" "Wait!" "Now!" in circus-font on one side and a picture of the artist at his Bar Mitzvah on the other, becomes a monument to varying levels of insecurity. Liebowitz's pun on the phrase "gain weight now"—itself a statement that utterly contradicts the societal obsession with physical fitness and weight loss—resonates humorously with the image of the dumpy young man, who looks suitably depressed about being an awkward adolescent participating in an intimidating rite of passage.

Michael Smith's video *OYMA (Outstanding Young Men of America)*, 1996, takes its point of departure from another symbolic and potentially awkward event that marks the transition from adolescence to adulthood. Smith's narrative follows the artist's nomination to OYMA, an organization like "Who's Who" that compiles biographical indices based on peer recommendations. The vague distinction is made all the more dubious by Smith's lonesome celebration of the recognition. "Strutting his funky stuff" as night descends on his party of one, Smith ponders the future with deadpan precision. Underscoring the emptiness of such unqualified public acceptance recalls the Woody Allen quote: "Eternal nothingness is fine if you happen to be dressed for it."[7] Smith's deluded character is in the tradition of the cinematic fool whose idealized self-image is fundamentally at odds with that projected to others and who is thus doomed to failure.

Many artists in recent years have explored aspects of the pathetic or failure in their work, appreciating humanity at its most vulnerable and abject. Peter Land's work deals with a more literal and slapstick representation of failure

William Pope.L
Foraging #3 (The Air Itself) **from the series** ***Black Domestic*****, 1995–98**
Cibachrome print
52 x 40 inches, framed
(132.1 x 101.6 cm)
Courtesy of the artist and Projectile Gallery

Susan Smith-Pinelo
Sometimes**, 2001**
Single-channel video with sound
4 minutes, 58 seconds
Courtesy of Fusebox, Washington, D.C.

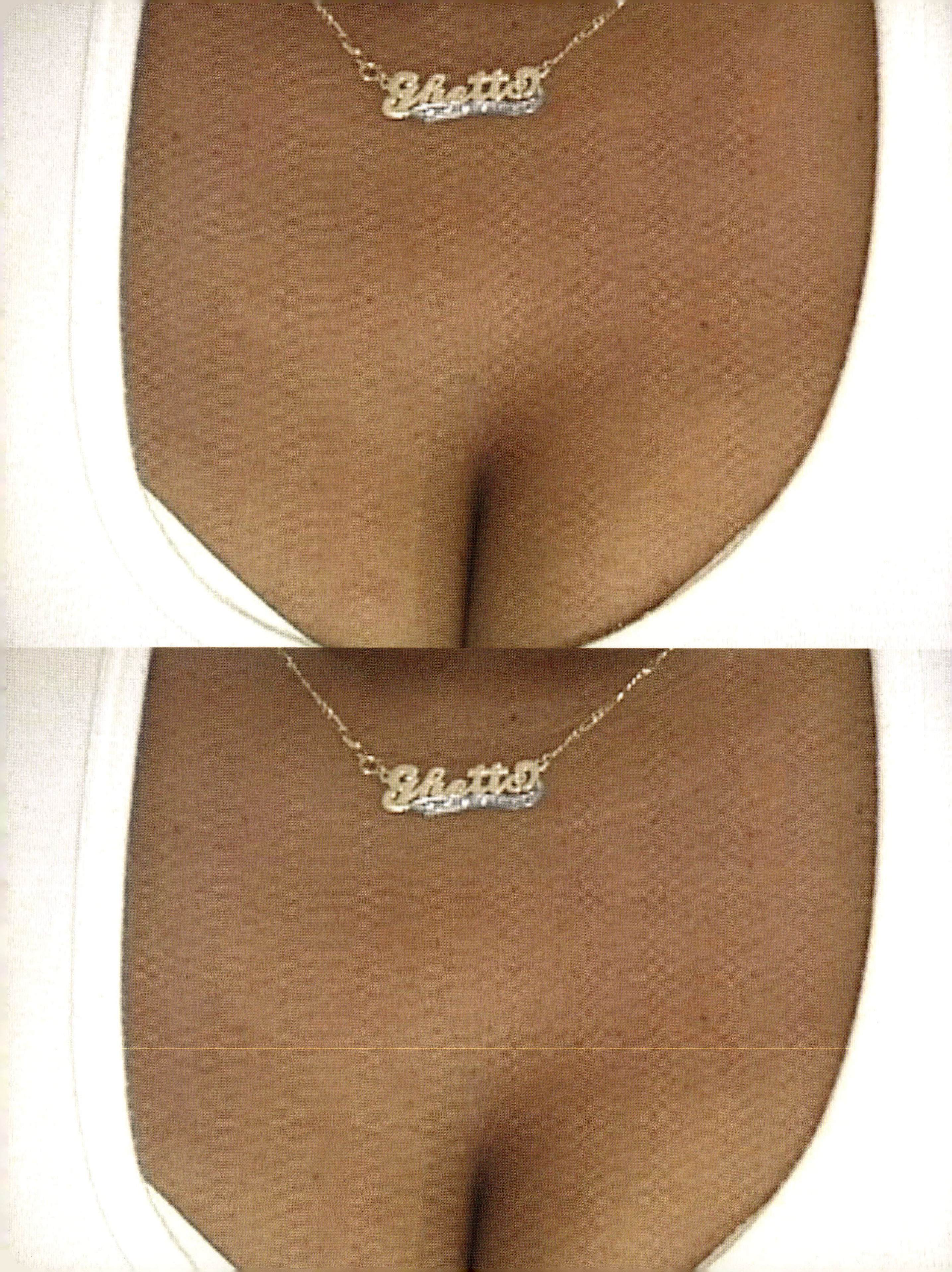
Ghetto
Ghetto

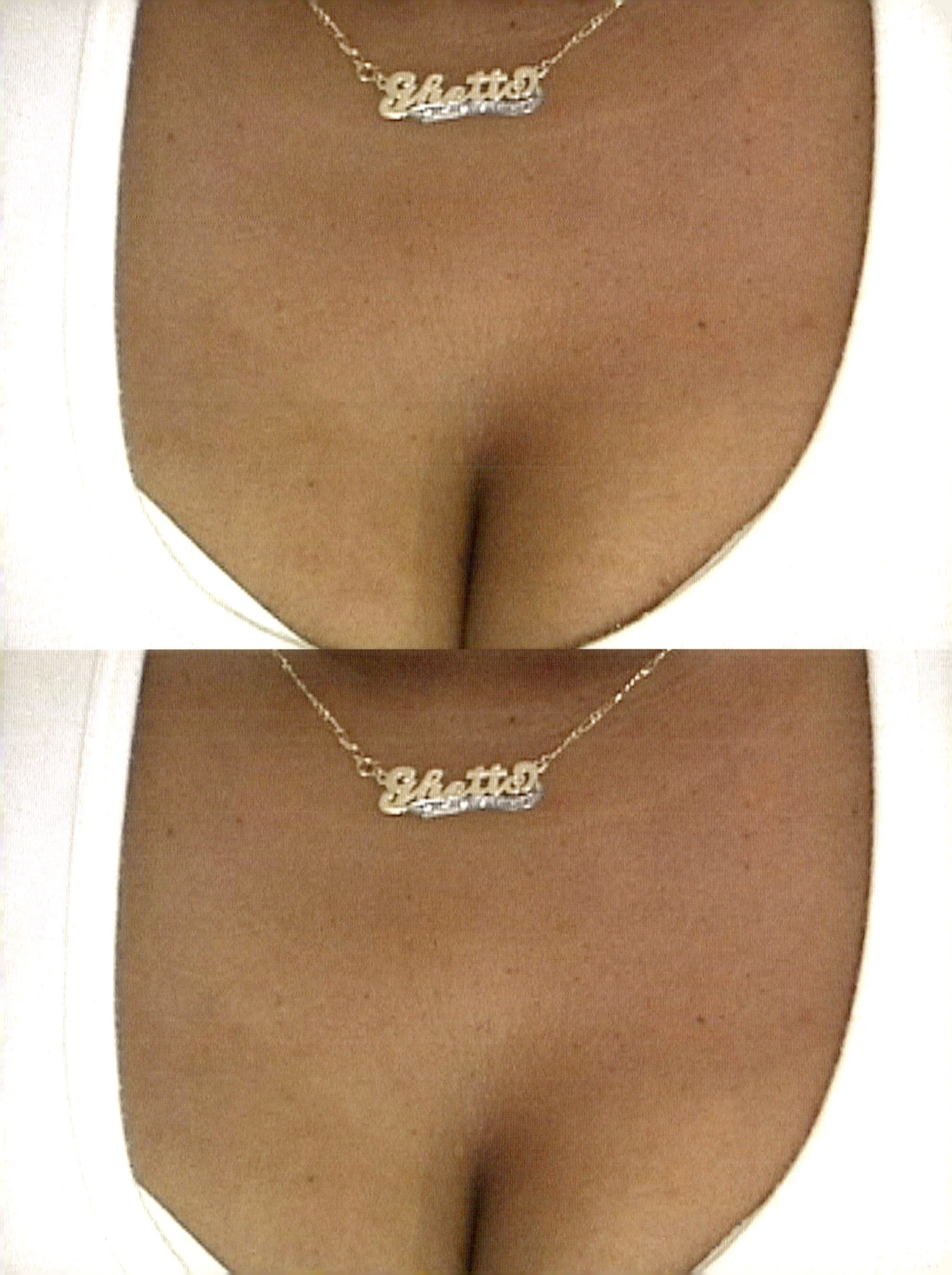
Ghetto
Ghetto

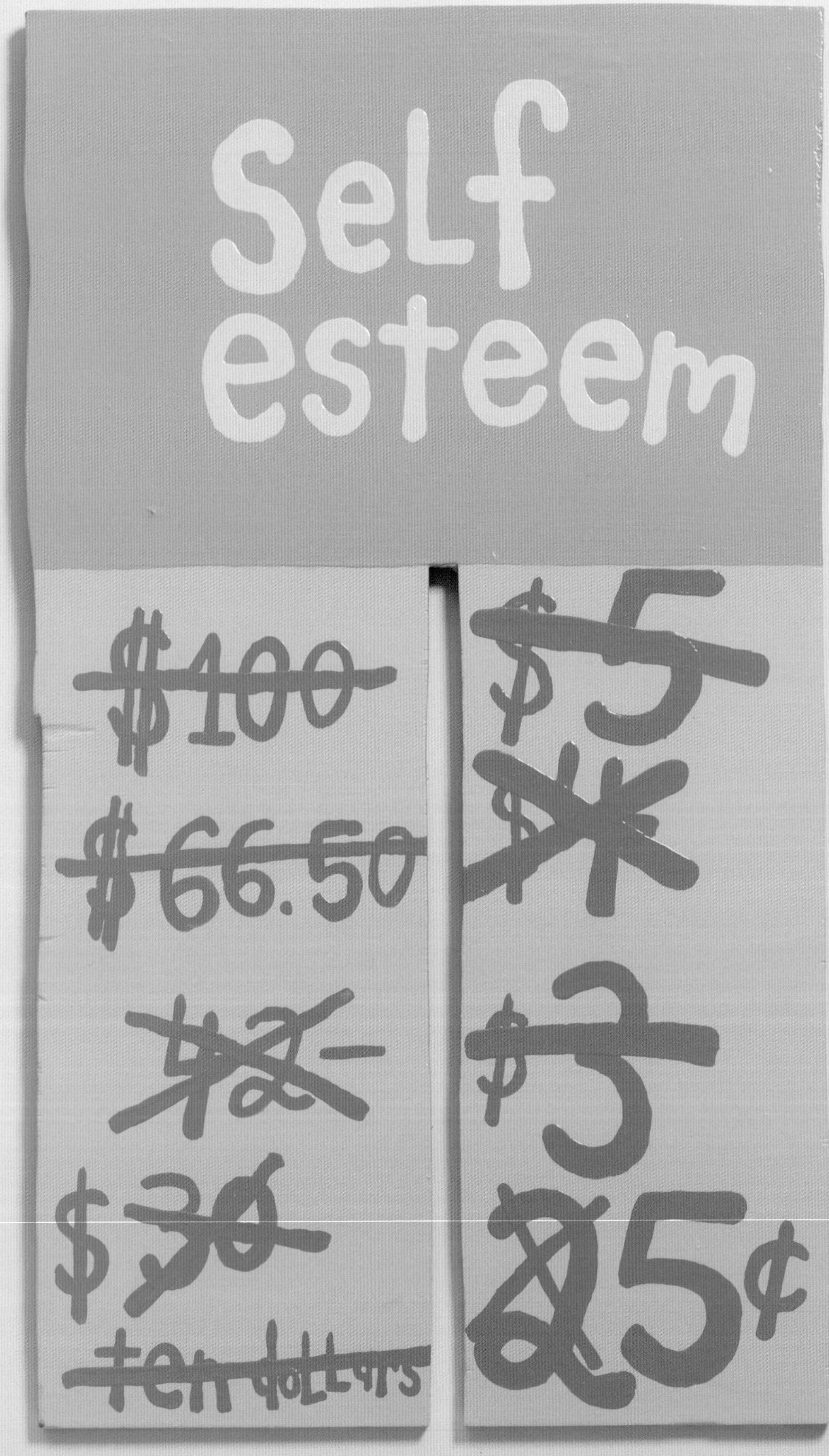

Self esteem

~~$100~~

~~$66.50~~

~~$12-~~

~~$30~~

~~ten dollars~~

~~$5~~

~~$4~~

~~$3~~

~~2~~5¢

in his use of physical humor to symbolize larger notions of humanity's frailty. *Pink Space*, 1995, is a video in which the artist, dressed as a showman/comedian in a violet-blue lamé tuxedo jacket, repeatedly attempts to take the microphone and commence his act, only to fall off the stage every time. The performer's frustration moves the viewer from a gut reaction of laughter at this classic bit of physical, falling down humor to more serious considerations for the man's well-being. As Land himself comments: "The work is about my feeling of failure in my attempts at establishing meaning on a personal as well as an artistic level. The feeling that I'm expected to say or to do something meaningful; to interfere, but that the mental apparatus needed for such an act has collapsed or evaporated and I'm left dumb."[8] Land's repeated pratfalls thus create an initially comic effect that belies a much deeper and more affecting psychology and emotional intent.

The slapstick element in *Pink Space* and other works by Land is shared in the work of other artists in the exhibition. Rodney Graham's ravishing 35 millimeter film, *Vexation Island*, 1997, slowly builds to a climax that is a classic cliché of physical humor—a pirate marooned on an island who is unexpectedly hit on the head by a falling coconut. In this film, time plays a critical factor in deferring the "punch line" until after slow pans of the lush tropical landscape. These seduce the audience to suspend its recognition of a classic setup that has been used by generations of humorists to parody the equally well-worn literary theme of man vs. nature. Like the coconut-on-the-head gag enacted in Graham's film, the pie fight is a timeless sight gag employed by Belarussian artist Alexej Koschkarow in his video *Tortenschlacht (Pie Fight), 2003*. Documenting a staged pie fight in a banquet hall among a large group of elegantly dressed participants, who are watched from behind velvet ropes by an equally well-dressed audience, *Tortenschlacht* sets up a situation in which the folly of high society is literally mirrored by the outlandish behavior of one half of its representatives. The utter excess of edible material stuff tossed about in the resulting melee is part Three Stooges, part Hermann Nitsch performance. Although pure slapstick, Koschkarow's pie fight suggests a more serious questioning of social values and priorities in the tradition of the infamous Belgian "pie-throwing anarchist" Noel Godin, whose carefully vetted celebrity targets tend to have an overly severe sense of self-importance and a limited sense of irony. A more cartoonish version of physical humor—in the sense of a Looney Tunes character like Wile E. Coyote—is found in Tom Friedman's *Untitled* image from 1996, showing a comically oversized man-shaped hole in a landscape as if someone had fallen from the sky. Re-creating this classic animated cartoon moment to appear strangely authentic not only provides a sense of humorous displacement but also executes a subtle spoof on the heroics of Land Art figures such as Michael Heizer and Robert Smithson. Friedman's 1993 black-and-white image of a man (the artist) improbably stuck flat, face down against a ceiling is predicated on the same Saturday morning, TV cartoon-oriented defiance of gravity. However, minus the narrative antics and colorful display of its Pop cultural referent, the image is emptied of its initially comedic affect and replaced with a more bleak and existential sensibility, conjuring a wry smile and an anxious guffaw.

Cary Liebowitz

***Self Esteem 100 Dollars, Reduced to 5 Cents*, 1995**
Latex house paint on wood
30 x 17½ inches (76.2 x 44.5 cm)
Collection of Scott Lorinsky; courtesy Andrew Kreps Gallery, New York

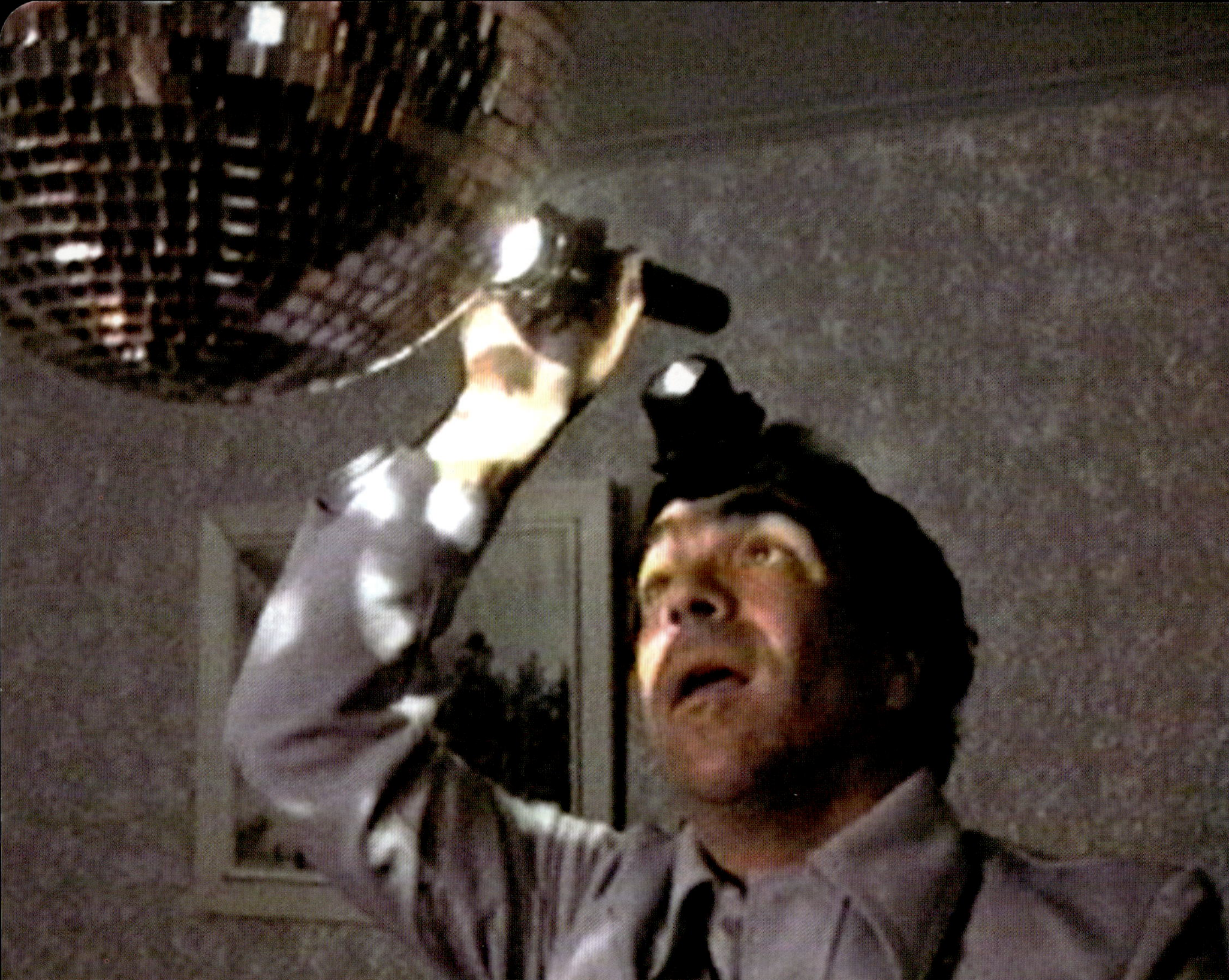

Michael Smith

OYMA (Outstanding Young Men of America), 1996
Single-channel video with sound
9 minutes, 23 seconds
Courtesy Electronic Arts Intermix, New York

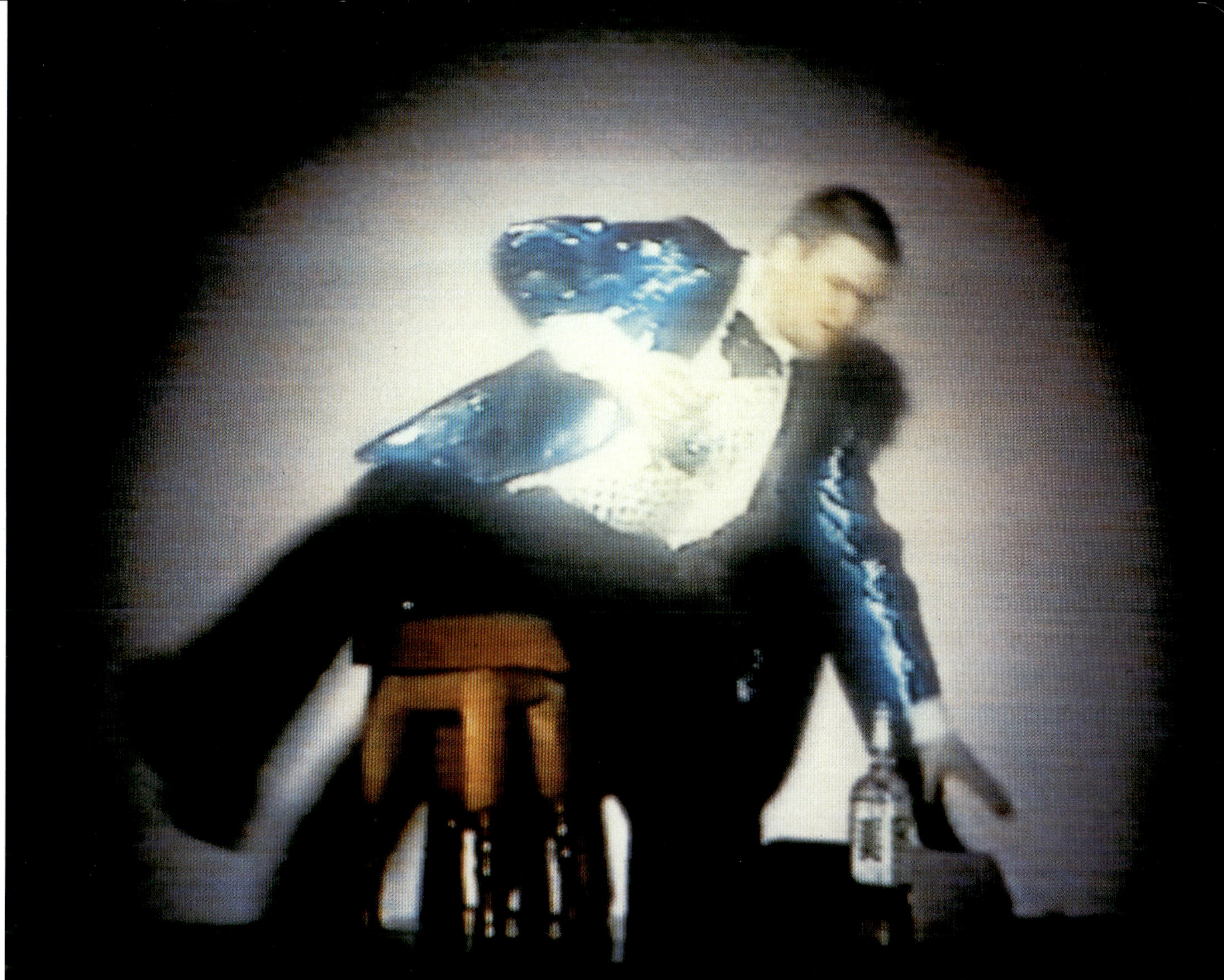

Peter Land

Pink Space, 1995
Single-channel video with sound
17 minutes, 35 seconds
Collection of the artist; courtesy Galleri Nicolai Wallner, Copenhagen

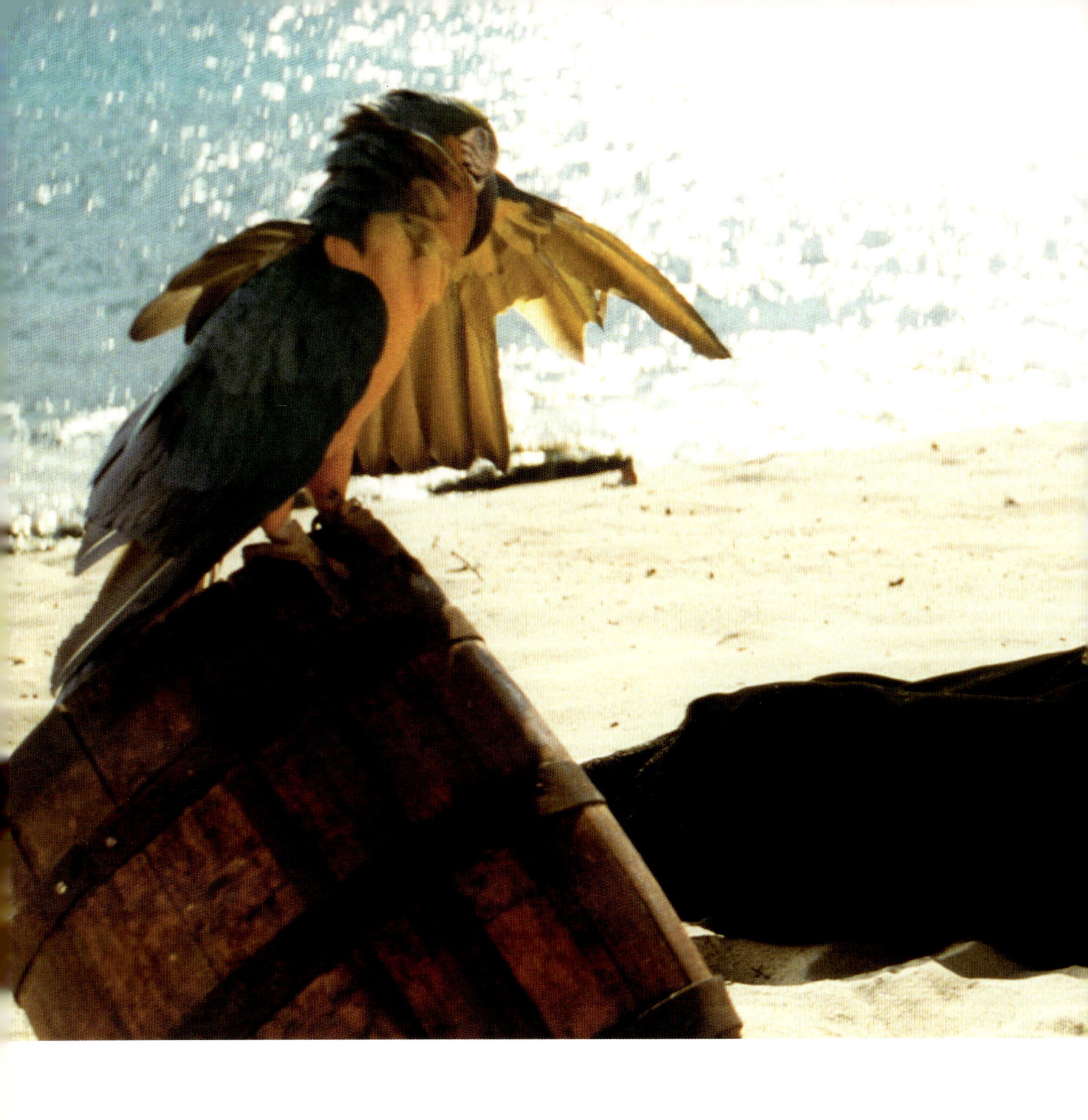

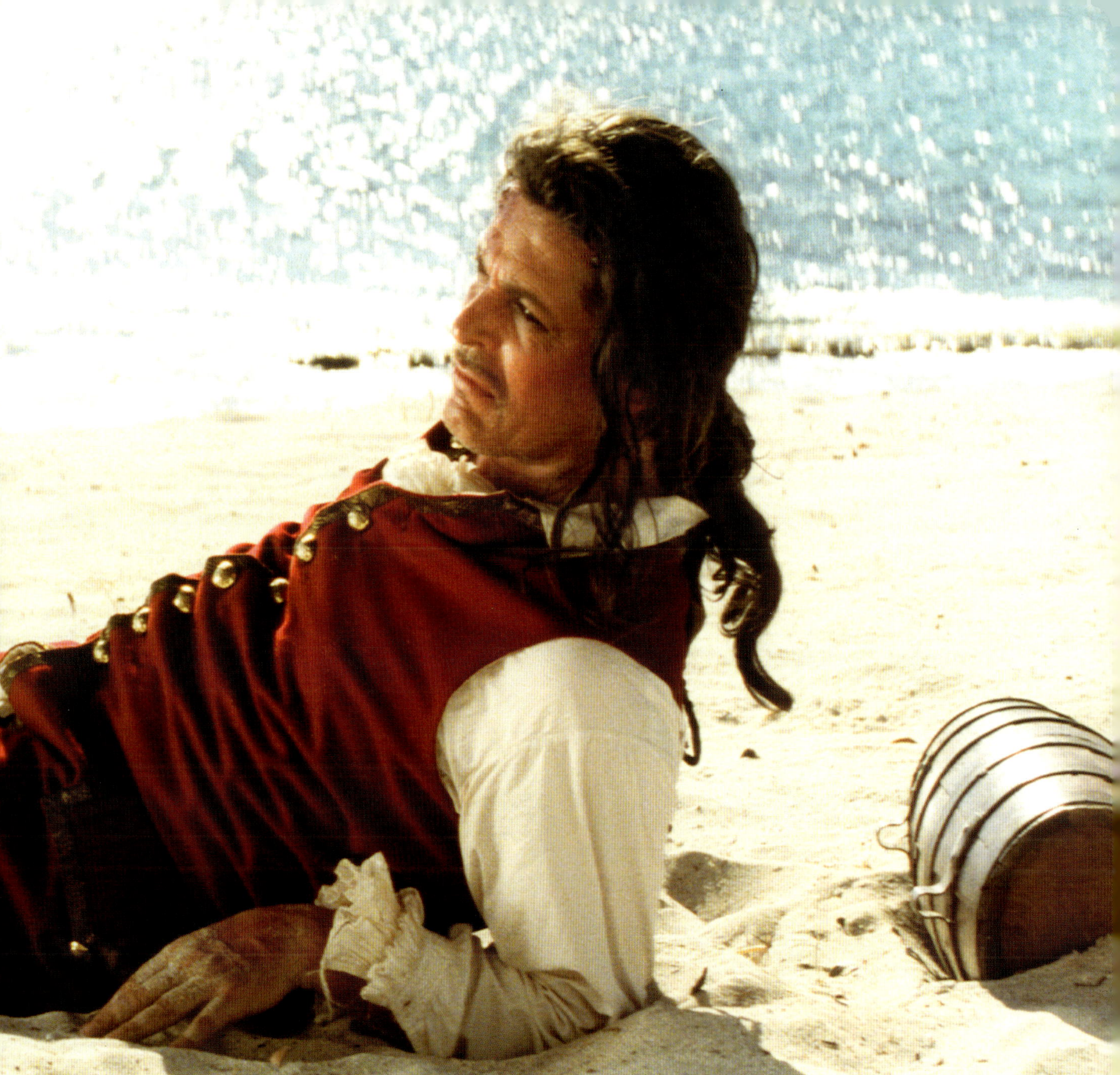

Rodney Graham

Vexation Island, 1997
Single-channel video with sound from 35mm film transferred to laser disc
9 minutes, continuous loop
Collection of the artist;
courtesy Donald Young Gallery, Chicago

Alexej Koschkarow

Tortenschlacht (Pie Fight), 2003
Single-channel video with sound
13 minutes
Collection of the artist; courtesy
Jablonka Lühn, Cologne

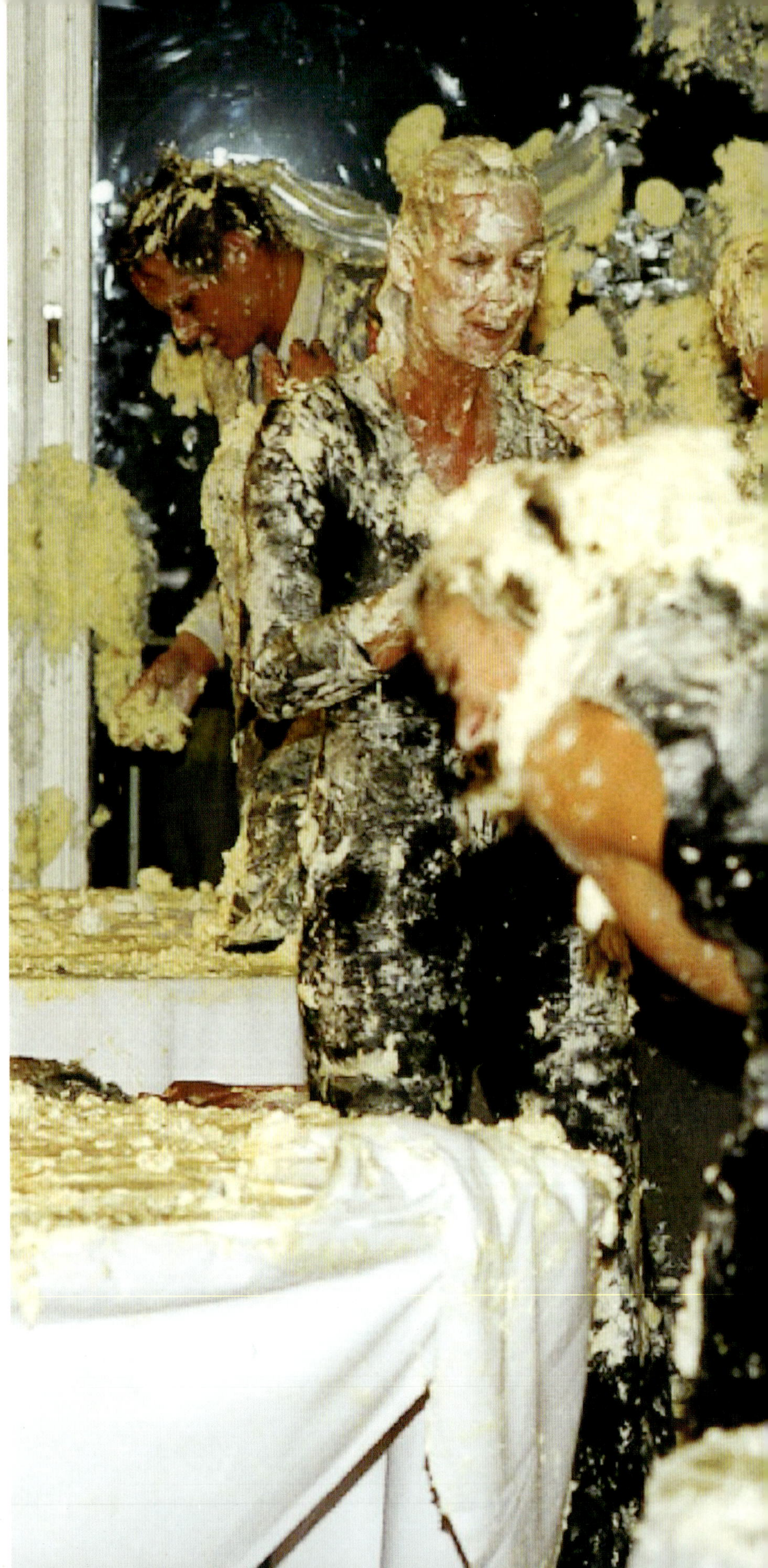

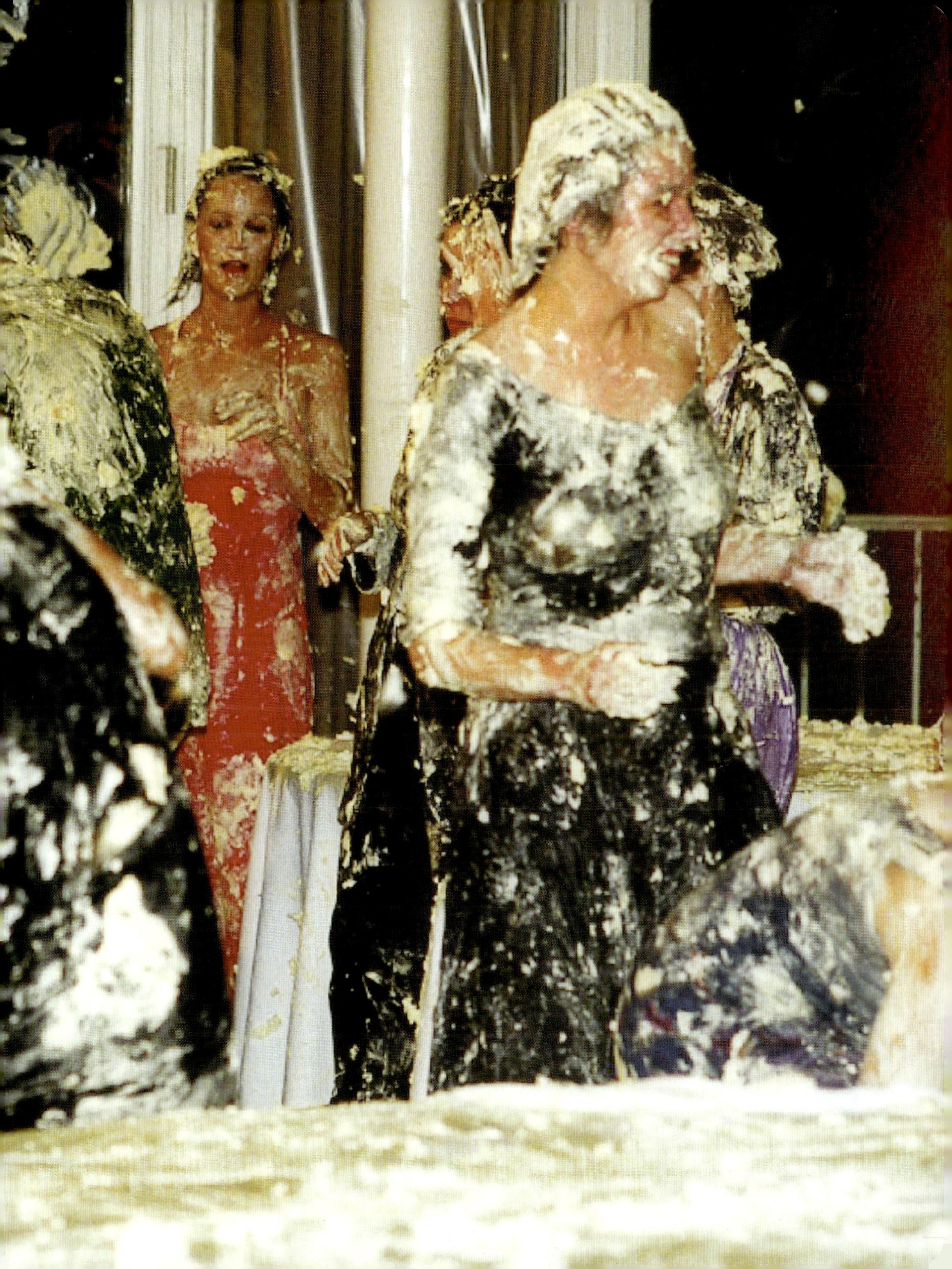

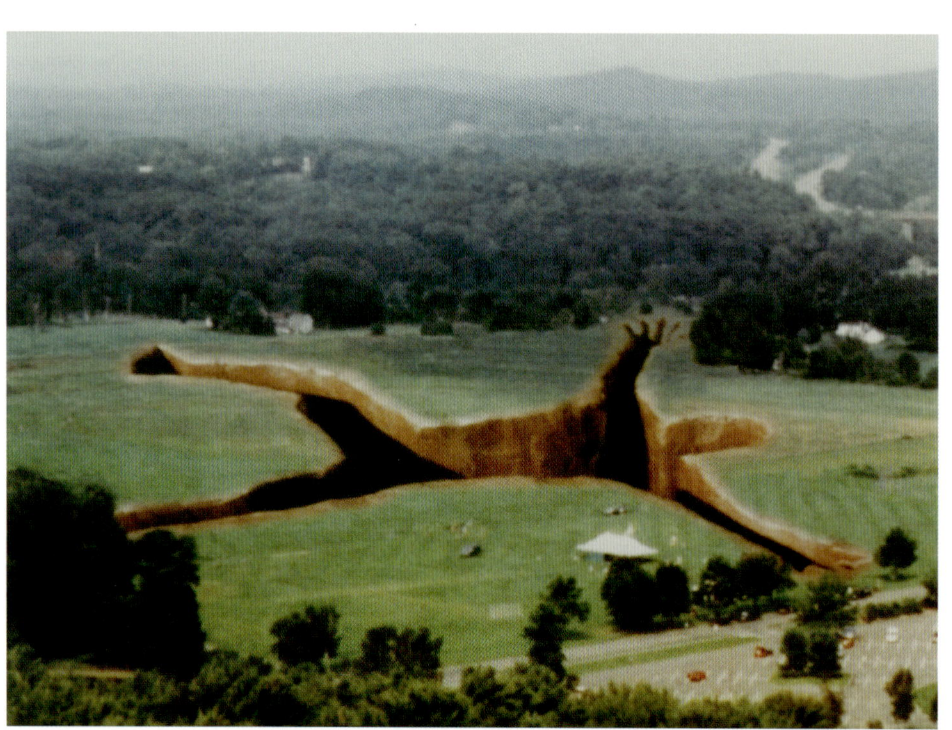

In much of his work of the mid-1990s Martin Kersels uses his extremely oversized body in comedic actions which he documents and then re-presents in serial photographs. *Tossing a Friend (Melinda)*, 1996, for example, shows three views of the artist throwing a diminutive female friend in the air, an activity made humorous through the drastic contrast in size between the two figures. The very action staged in the sequence suggests a more symbolic representation of gender imbalances in society. By literally enacting and exaggerating unequal power relationships between men and women, Kersels holds both sides of the argument up to ridicule. Other works by Kersels depict the artist falling down in public places—a gesture at once pathetic and comic and reminiscent of artistic precedents such as work by Bas Jan Ader and Bruce Nauman.

Tom Friedman
***Untitled*, 1996**
Cibachrome print
3 x 6⅛ inches (7.6 x 15.6 cm)
Private collection;
courtesy Neal Meltzer Fine Art, Inc.

If Kersels's work draws humor from overemphasizing his corpulence, Tony Tasset and Dana Schutz's works flaunt what are considered the more embarrassing or disgusting aspects of our physical being. Tasset's *I Peed In My Pants*, 1994, is a life-size self-portrait with his arms folded and smiling with a look of smug satisfaction—a frame of mind ridiculously at odds with his urine-soaked pants leg. Tasset flips a humiliating occurrence typically associated with either the very young or the very old into a comedic moment by displacing the accident onto a seemingly confident adult, who one would assume would have more control over his bodily functions. Dana Schutz's sneeze paintings use the visceral quality of paint to simulate the explosion of mucus from the nose in the action of sneezing. A sight gag involving bodily fluids—a mainstay in adolescent humor—is thus crossed with a formal exploration of the material quality of paint on the surface of the canvas. Schutz in essence creates a clever send-up of the fetishization of the gesture of the artist's hand in manipulating material, turning an aesthetic virtue into something disgusting and repugnant. Lawrence Seward's *Untitled* sculpture from 2000 exaggerates the simultaneous fear of embarrassment and repulsion that bodily fluids inspire by depicting a figure who has fallen face down into a large pool of nameless white goo. The unfashionable clothing worn by the figure suggests that he may be somewhat of a nerd, relating him to the comic mainstay of the hapless anti-heroic fool, or nebbish in Jewish humor, who is visited upon by one slapstick calamity after the next. Like others in the genre, Seward's nebbish connects to universal feelings of inadequacy and vulnerability, while the primordial slime in which he is mired suggests a frustrated search for meaning in our day-to-day grind.

Sight Gags and Other Shenanigans

Erwin Wurm's physical humor involves the placement of human figures with objects and settings that bring out the absurd and ironic elements of our relationship to the world or to one another. In *Looking for a Bomb 3* from the series *Instructions on How to Be Politically Incorrect*, 2002–03, for example, a man is shown sticking his arm through the fly of another man's pants up

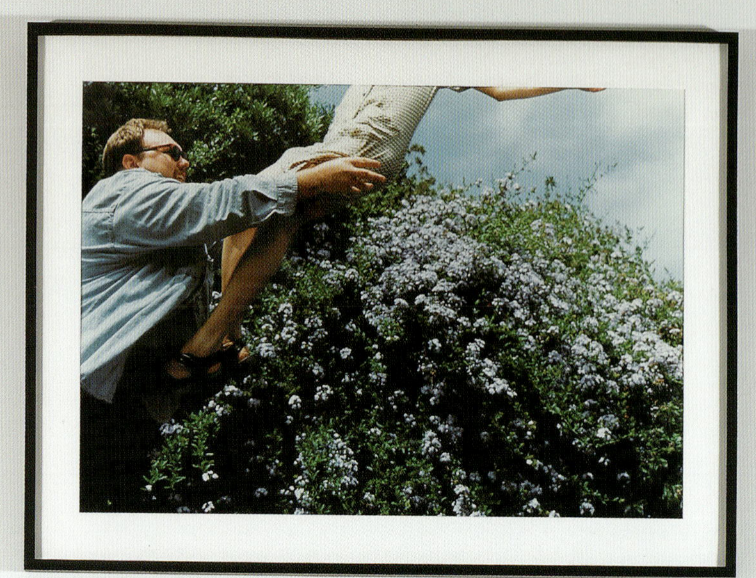
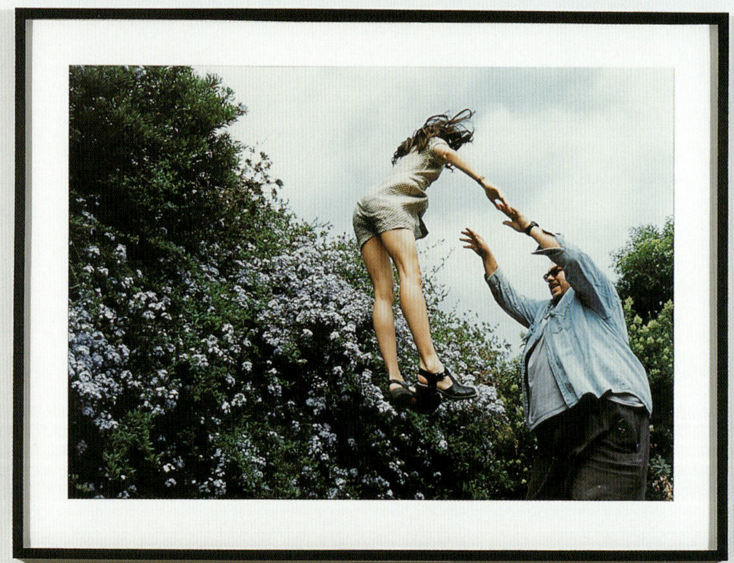
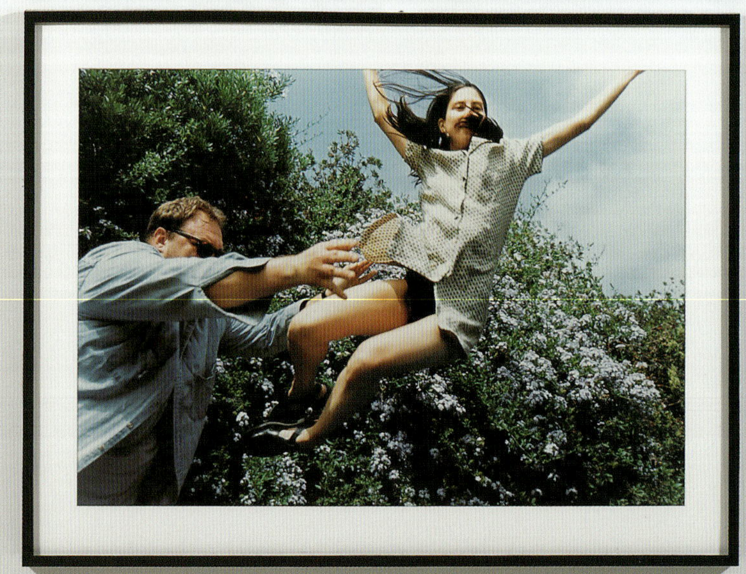

Tony Tasset

***I Peed in My Pants*, 1994**
Cibachrome print
83¼ x 38¼ inches framed (211.5 x 97.2 cm)
Collection of Refco Group, Ltd.

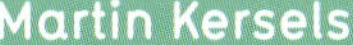

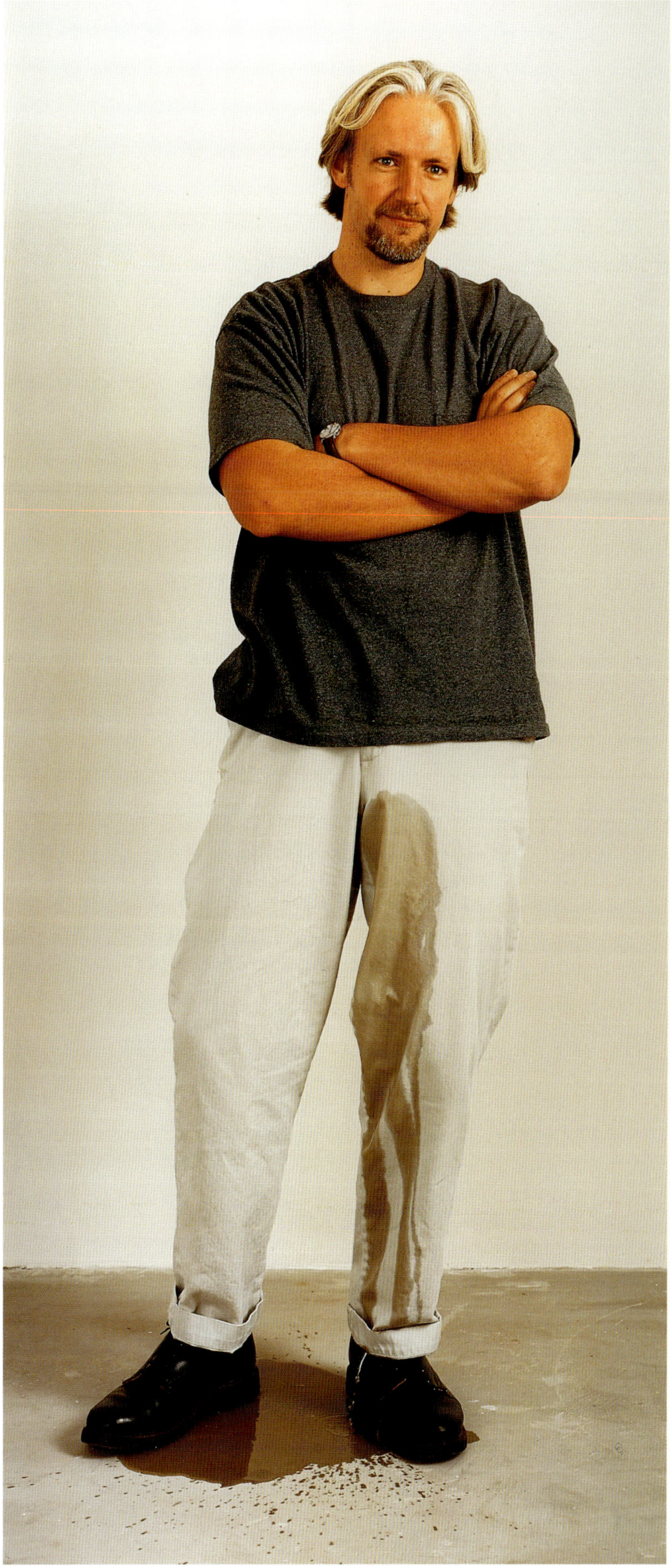

Martin Kersels

***Tossing a Friend (Melinda) (1, 2, and 3)*, 1996**
Three Cibachrome prints
Each: 34½ x 46½ inches framed (87.6 x 118.1 cm)
Collection of Burt Aaron, Detroit, Michigan

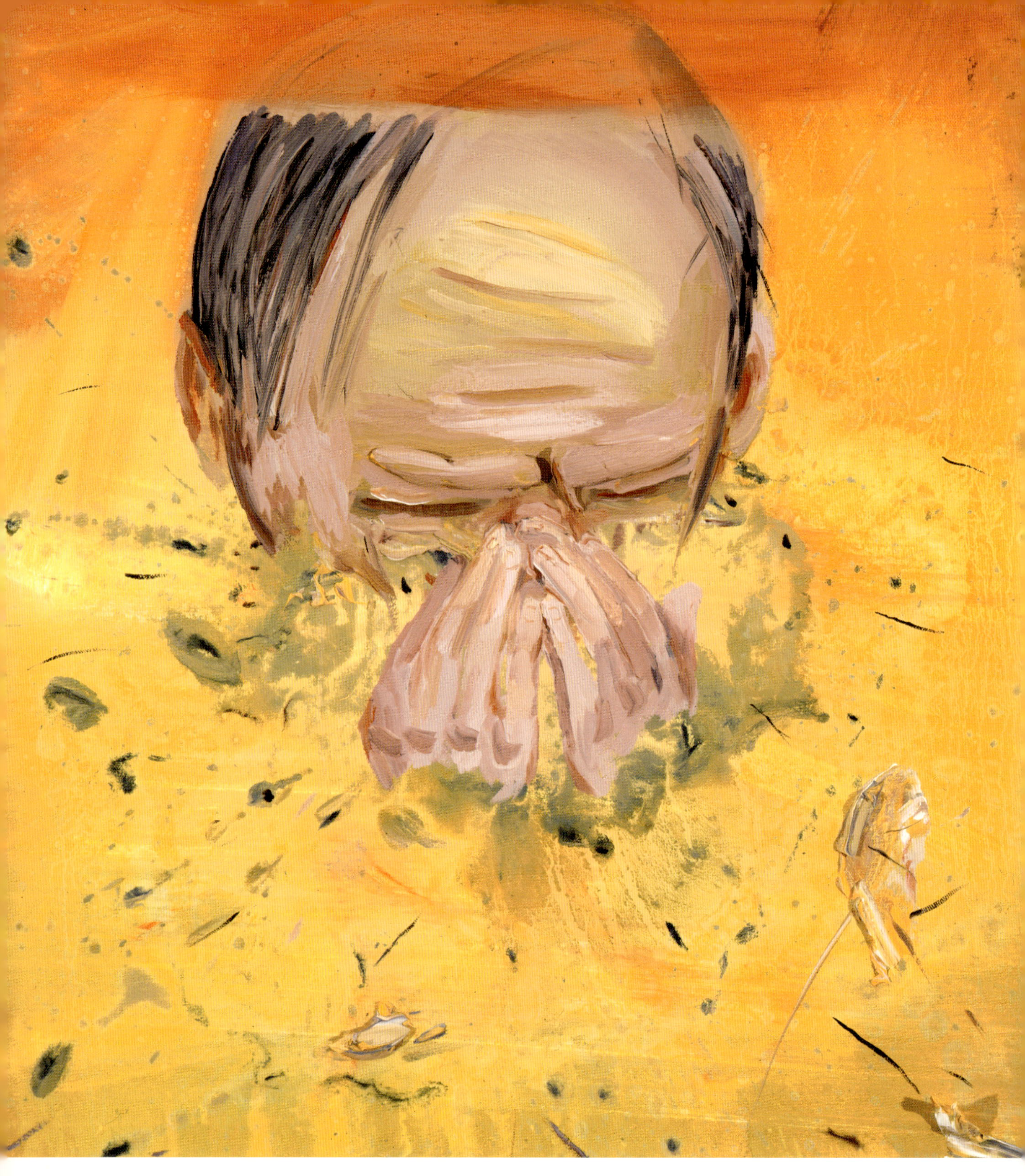

to his elbow—an action more in keeping with a sexual advance than a professional method of searching an individual were it not for the ridiculous improbability of such a thorough exploration of the man's trousers. The work assumes a dark comedic relationship to the anti-terrorist security measures taken around the world (most noticeably in the United States) in the wake of the attacks of September 11th—especially in terms of their impingement on civil liberties. Wurm lampoons our paranoia about terrorism and the absurd points to which society has striven to secure itself against possible threat by invading individual privacy and trampling human dignity regardless of social, cultural, or personal "sensitivities." The artist thus flips the socially curative but empty and ineffectual notion of "sensitivity training" towards the more subversive but accurate description of security procedures as "lessons on how to be politically incorrect."

Physical exaggeration as a mainstay of comedy in the entertainment industry is addressed in the works of both David Robbins and John Waters. Robbins has devoted much of his visual art practice and writing to an exploration of comedy and is currently working on an alternate history of comedy in America. His *Self-Parody*, 1993, features three rows of appropriated publicity photographs of famous comedians of yesteryear such as W.C. Fields, Lucille Ball, and Groucho Marx. All of the figures in these images adopt facial expressions in keeping with their comedic persona, cultivating the role of the fool or jester at the expense of a more dignified physical appearance. The title not only alludes to this form of self-deprecation but also to a previous work by Robbins titled *Talent*, 1986, for which he had nineteen artist friends (including Jeff Koons, Ashley Bickerton, and Cindy Sherman) pose for the kind of "head shots" used by actors and actresses. While that work was itself a parody of fine artists' status as celebrities and "entertainers," *Self-Parody* adopts a form and structure identical to its predecessor to perform a further take on Robbins's own oeuvre.

Waters is best known as a filmmaker whose comedies feature an endless parade of bad taste and vulgar behavior. His work as an artist incorporates humor of a slightly less bawdy and more self-reflective sensibility than the gross-out ridiculousness of *Pink Flamingos* (1972) or *Female Trouble* (1974). His photograph, *In My Mind*, 1994, for example, presents as an imaginary self-portrait the Claymation figure of comedian Don Knotts in the role of Barney Fife. Waters has ironically commented: "I have always thought of Don Knotts as a sort of spiritual guru," observing his superficial resemblance to Knotts, who embodies the role of the quintessentially anti-heroic, nervous patsy. His self-effacing comparison with Fife's character upsets the venerated history of self-portraiture and accepted notions of the genre as a reflection of inner nobility and artistic introspection. *Visit Marfa*, 2003, is a mock circus poster promoting the late, preeminent Minimalist Donald Judd's compound in Texas. The poster, which reads in part "Take the Whole Family to Marfa, Texas," presents Judd's austere and ambitious project as a popular amusement. Other taglines such as "The Jonestown of Minimalism," ridicule the revisionist tendency to emphasize spirituality in

Dana Schutz
***Sneeze 2*, 2001**
Oil on canvas
20 x 19 inches (50.8 x 48.2 cm)
Private collection

relation to Minimalism and its interpretation. By promoting Judd's bastion of Minimalist purity like a three-ring circus, Waters takes a bit of air out of the hubris and grandeur of high art, humorously suggesting that the rarefied milieu of Minimalist art (itself often the target of jokes for its abstruseness) is an exhilarating entertainment. As a visual artist as well as a filmmaker, Waters also takes aim at the art world canon and establishment with which he himself identifies and thus directs his sardonic wit at himself.

Verbal Sallies, Wordplay, and Jokes

If Waters and Robbins utilize the Conceptual art format of the serial or multiple photograph, artists such as Stephanie Brooks, Kelly Mark, and Kay Rosen use the written or spoken word, stripping down the comedic gesture to linguistic games and turns of phrase. Brooks's work is characterized by subtle infiltrations into the signs and devices that structure our everyday life as well as language in general. In her 2002 series *Politeness Strategy*, she offers the viewer a choice of three possible answers to a simple statement—for example, "You have a nice day/ass/attitude." Her witty representation of an instinctually unconscious thought process as a simple visual equation prompts a unique consideration of how language and socialized behavior interrelate. Mark's sound work *I really should...1,000*, 2002, features the artist dryly stating patently obvious reminders to herself: "I really should eat out less" or "I really should take a shower." Her bland delivery of this seemingly endless litany (a wonderfully repentant variation on Shrigley's "From now I will do exactly as I am told") enhances the inherently comic prospect of repetitious self-admonishment ad infinitum. Mark's video *Reuben*, 2003, derives its comic impact from the lack of sound in its deadpan documentation of a young man having a very earnest conversation with a work of figurative public sculpture. Voyeuristic urges are satisfied by Mark's distant observation of the demented monologue, even as this distance frustrates our intrinsic curiosity to hear the "conversation."

The droll word play in Rosen's paintings usually involves a deliberate and strategic misspelling or visual shift to create a sense of linguistic double take. For example, in *Double Whammy*, 1993, the extra "W" and "M" enable a humorously self-reflexive re-reading of this odd yet common phrase. *Aunt Bea*, 1994, moves progressively from the world of insects—"Queen Ant" and "Queen Bee"—to the world of television sit-coms—Aunt Bea from the Andy Griffith Show of the 1960s. The motherly nature of the television character is contrasted with the appearance of the term Queen Bee (which is typically used to describe a diva-like woman) while the color scheme—black bands of text on a yellow background— evokes the color of a bumblebee.

A quite different incorporation of text as a comedic gesture in the work of art is found in the joke-oriented works of Richard Prince and Laura Nova. Prince's ongoing series of *White Paintings* feature a layering of silkscreened fragments of cartoons appropriated from *The New Yorker* or other

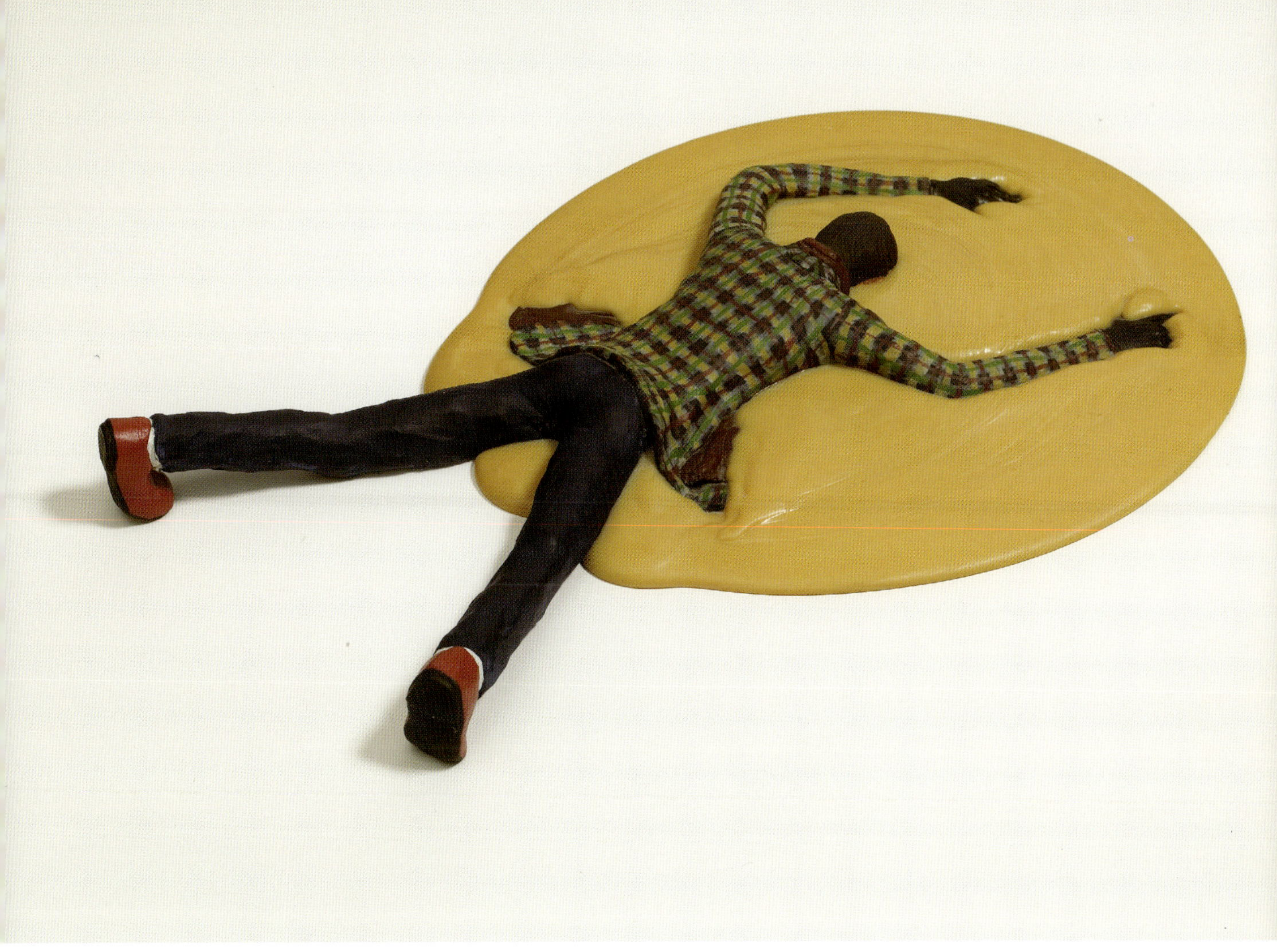

Lawrence Seward

Untitled, 2000
Rubber, metal, plaster, and acrylic paint
2½ x 17 x 25½ inches
(6.4 x 43.2 x 64.8 cm)
Collection of Erin H. McKinnon, New York

Erwin Wurm

Looking for a Bomb 3, from the series ***Instructions on How to Be Politically Incorrect***, 2003
Cibachrome print mounted on aluminum under Plexiglas
50 x 73 inches (126 x 184 cm)
Collection of the artist;
courtesy Jack Hanley Gallery, San Francisco

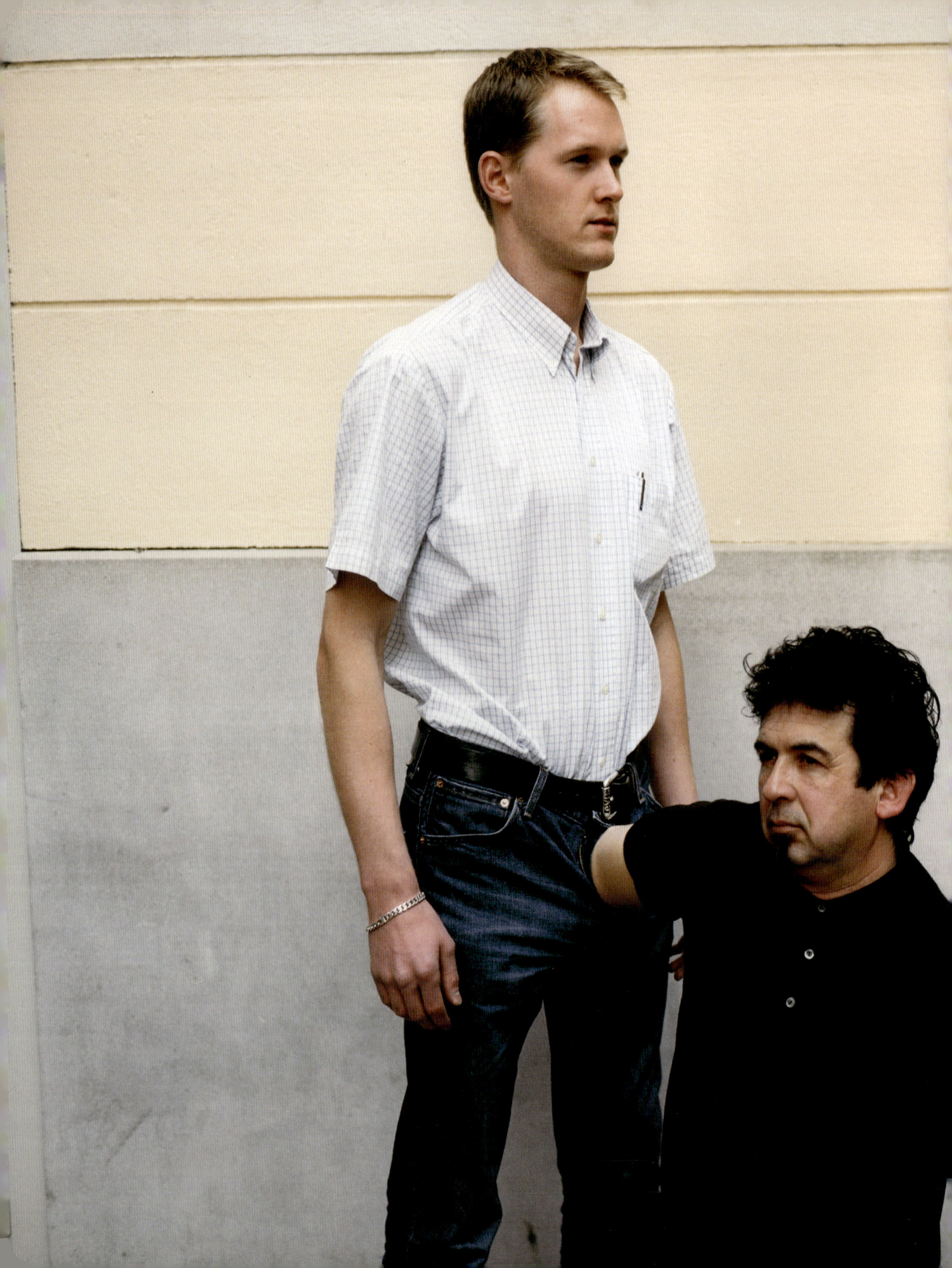

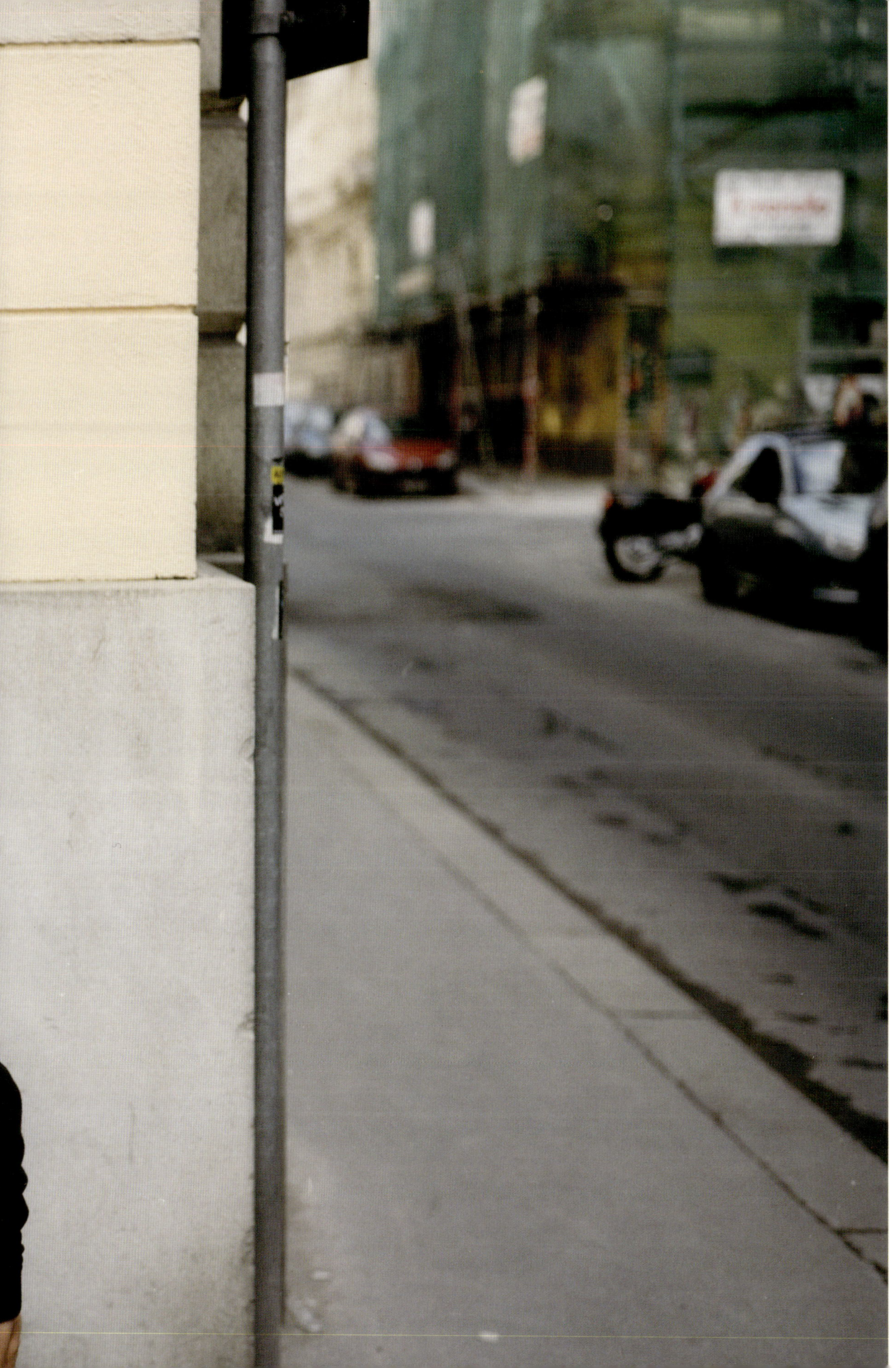

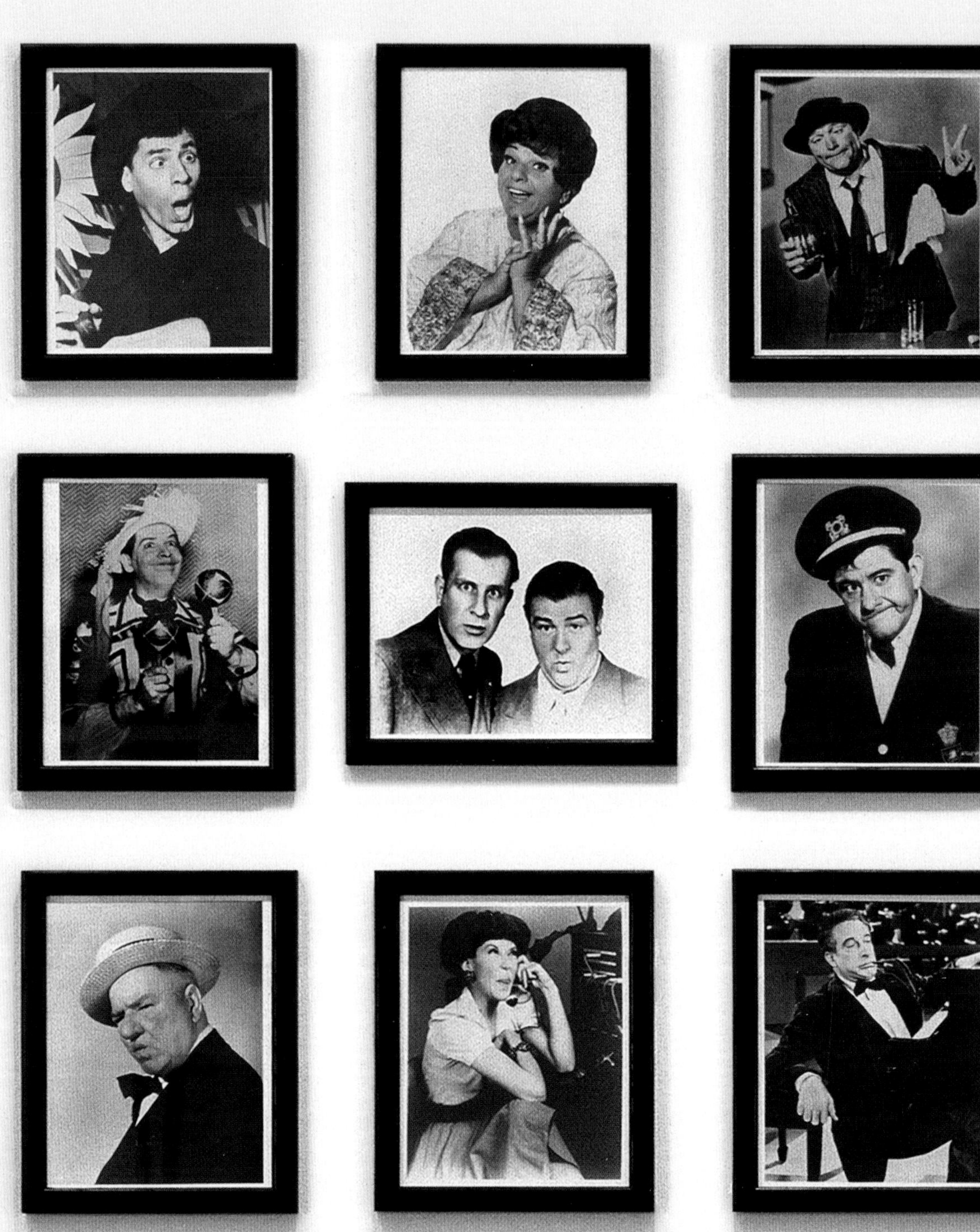

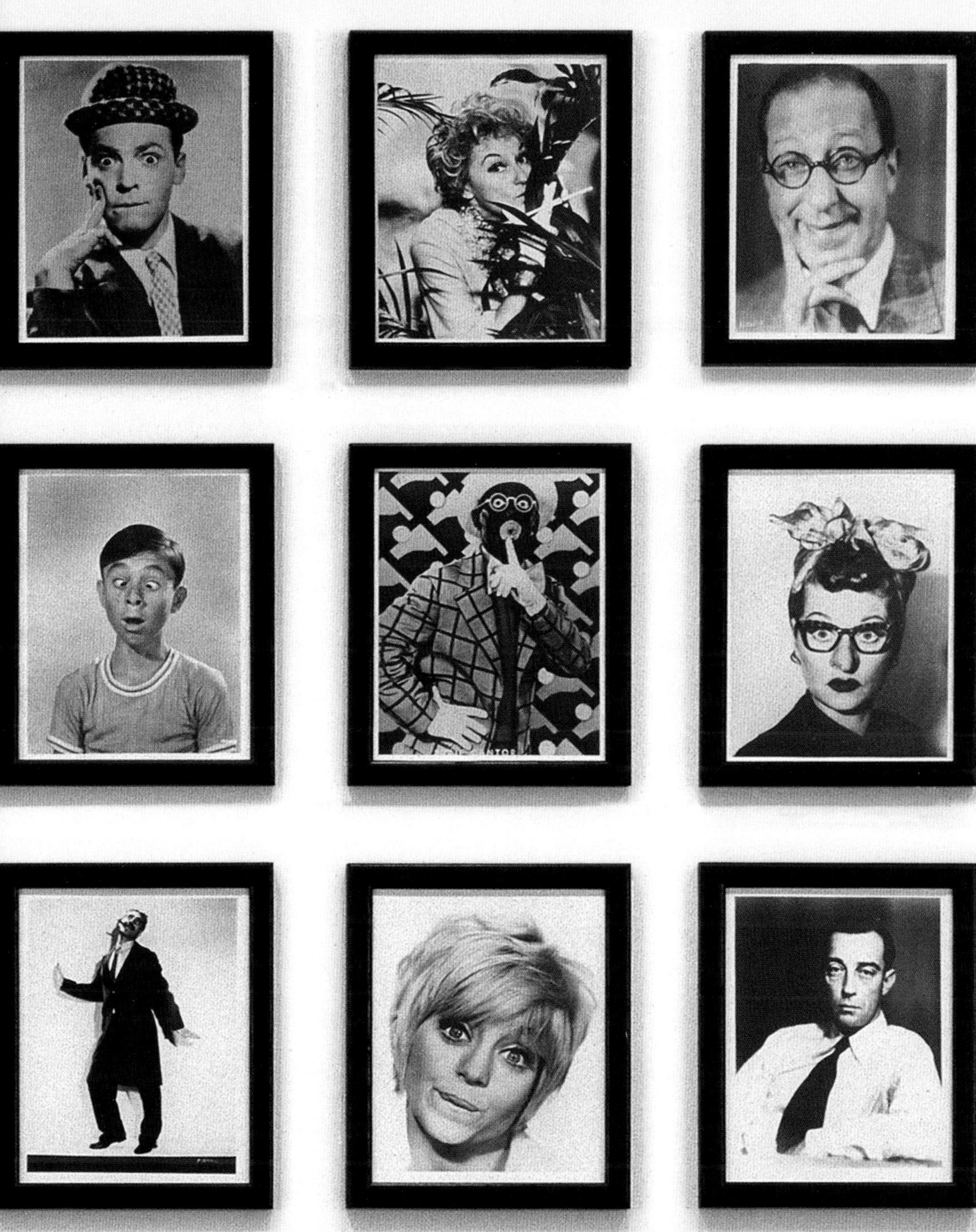

magazines and classic stand-up jokes. The jokes serve as either inappropriate captions or non sequiturs for the actions portrayed in the cartoons, thus altering the understanding of both elements. *Good News, Bad News*, 1989, bears a joke about a doctor giving bad news to his patient about his remaining life expectancy. The punch line is the good news – the doctor's latest sexual conquest – which has nothing to do with the patient's condition but literally satisfies the terms of the hackneyed set-up. As in his other *White Paintings*, Prince repeats and fragments the joke, displacing its comedic emphasis, thus diminishing the effect of the punch line and serving to render problematic the joke's characteristic use-value as a softly misogynistic form of bonding between straight men.

Nova's multimedia installation *On the Spot*, 2001, is a makeshift stand-up comedy stage complete with curtain backdrop, microphone, and a teleprompter that delivers jokes to viewers who choose to participate. Allowing time for the joke to be told, a rim shot (the cliché drum and cymbal riff that punctuates a stand-up joke, signaling the audience to, hopefully, laugh) goes off steadily while the participant's performance is transmitted via live-feed camera to a monitor resting at his or her feet. This last element serves as a displacing device much akin to the use of live-feed cameras and monitors in the installations of Bruce Nauman from the late-1960s/early-1970s. The constant distractions of this element and the continuous rim shot noise turn an initially humorous gallery experience into something more aggravating and unsettling.

Punch Line [or Conclusion]

The enduring role of the humorous or comedic in art comes as little surprise given the eternal need for humankind (and the art world) to take a critical step back from itself and seize psychological control over our shortcomings and failures. By inverting our day-to-day routine, the exigencies and imperatives that dictate our actions are put into a broader perspective and revealed to be more complex, more human, and sometimes funnier than we allow, or as is attributed to Buster Keaton, "Life is a tragedy when seen in close-up, but a comedy in long-shot." Demonstrated by the artists in *Situation Comedy*, the self-acknowledgment of our inner tramps, fools, and blunderers is both a disarming and liberating exercise. Particularly in our era of accelerated communication, when every word is parsed and interpreted often against intentions, it is crucial that the absurdity of life's conditions be verbalized and visualized through the wide-angle lens of humor. While comedy is often incorrectly viewed as a diversion from a more meaningful meditation on the state of things, voiced by the typically overused criticism that an artist or their work is a "one-liner" (the criticism is itself a one-liner), the artists and works that comprise *Situation Comedy* hopefully prove that the opposite is true. By engaging us through the comedic situation, these artists address aspects of ourselves and the world around us that lie beneath the surface and which may cut to the quick, leading us into

David Robbins

***Self-Parody*, 1993**
Gelatin silver prints
Eighteen parts overall. Seventeen parts, each 10 x 8 inches (25.4 x 20.3 cm); one part, 8 x 10 inches (20.3 x 25.4 cm)
Collection Museum of Contemporary Art, Chicago, gift of James Mark Pedersen

John Waters

***Visit Marfa*, 2003**
Offset print
30 x 22 in. (76.2 x 55.9 cm)
Collection of the artist and Marianne Boesky Gallery, New York

SEE DONALD JUDD'S BED!

EAT FOOD ALL THE SAME COLOR!

SCARE THE LOCALS!

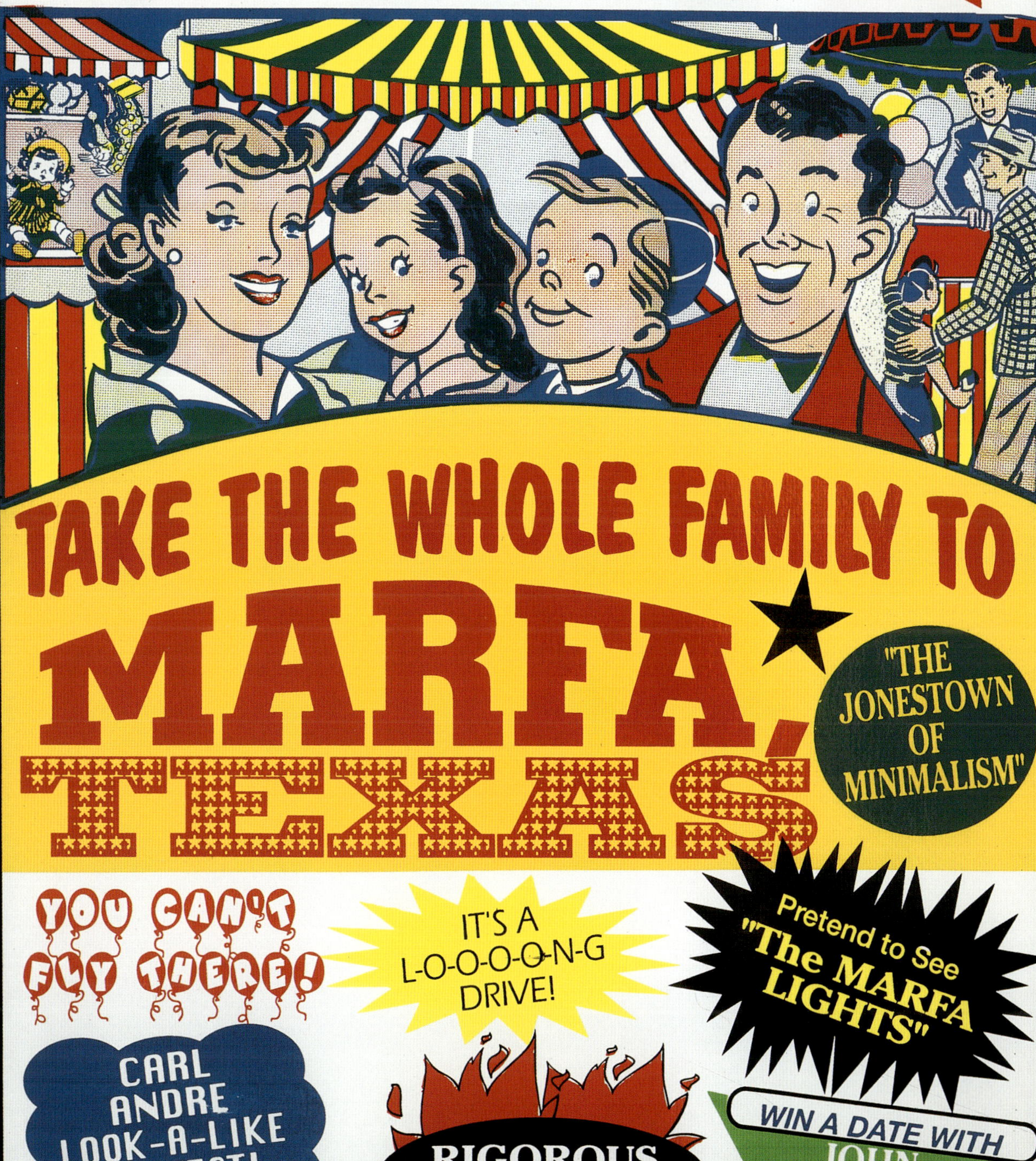

GLOBE POSTER PRINTING CORP. • 3705 BANK STREET • BALTIMORE, MD. 21224 • (410) 685-8787 • 2003

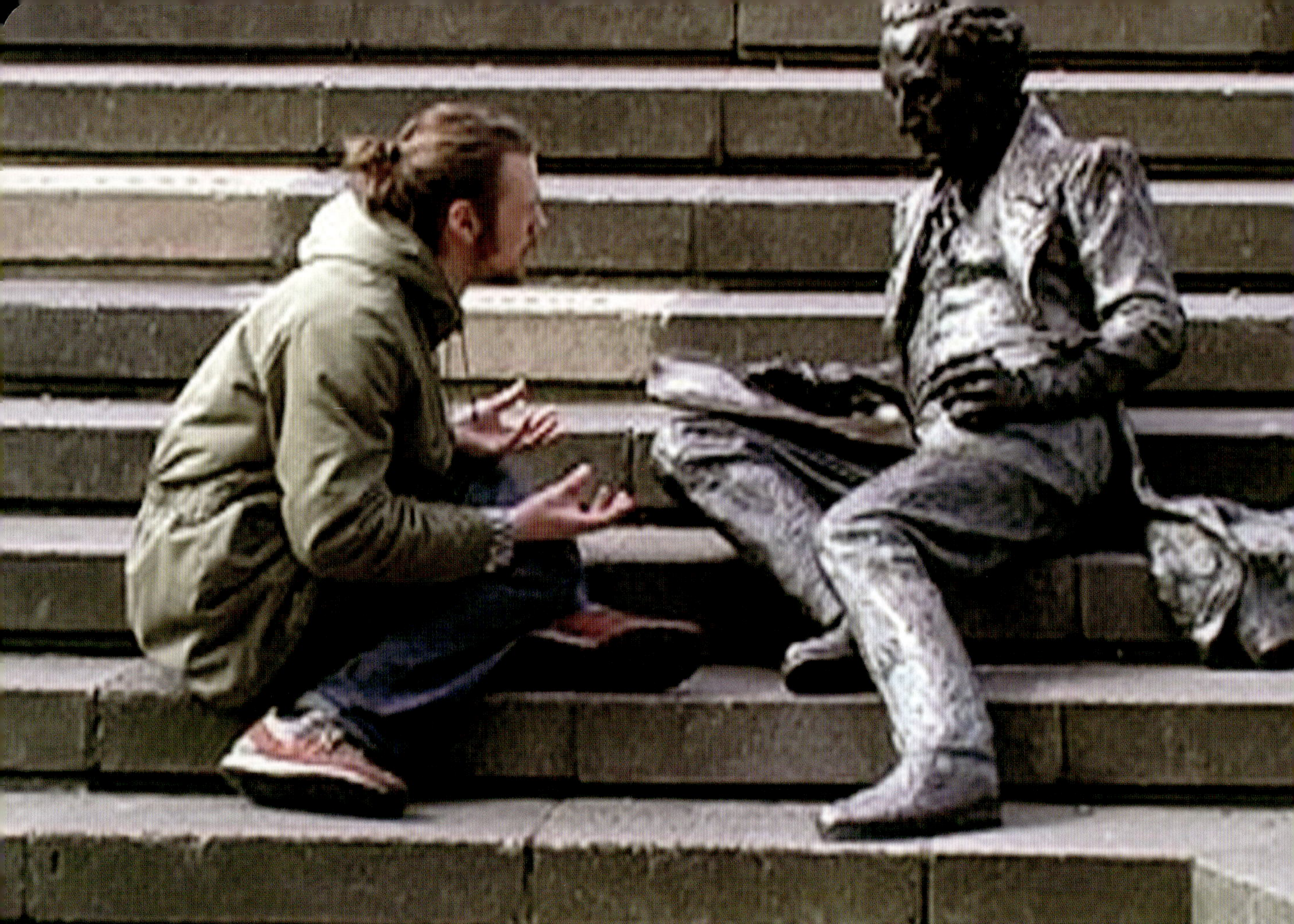

Kelly Mark
Reuben, 2003
Single-channel video
15 minutes, 30 seconds
Courtesy Wynick/Tuck Gallery, Toronto, and Tracey Lawrence Gallery, Toronto

Stephanie Brooks
Untitled from the ***Politeness Strategy series***, 2002
Enamel on etched zinc
5 x 7 in. (12.7 x 17.8 cm)
Collection of Cleve E. Carney

Kay Rosen
Double Whammy, 1993
Enamel sign paint on canvas
10 x 50 inches (25.4 x 127 cm)
Collection of Peter Norton, Santa Monica

Go { for it.
fuck yourself.

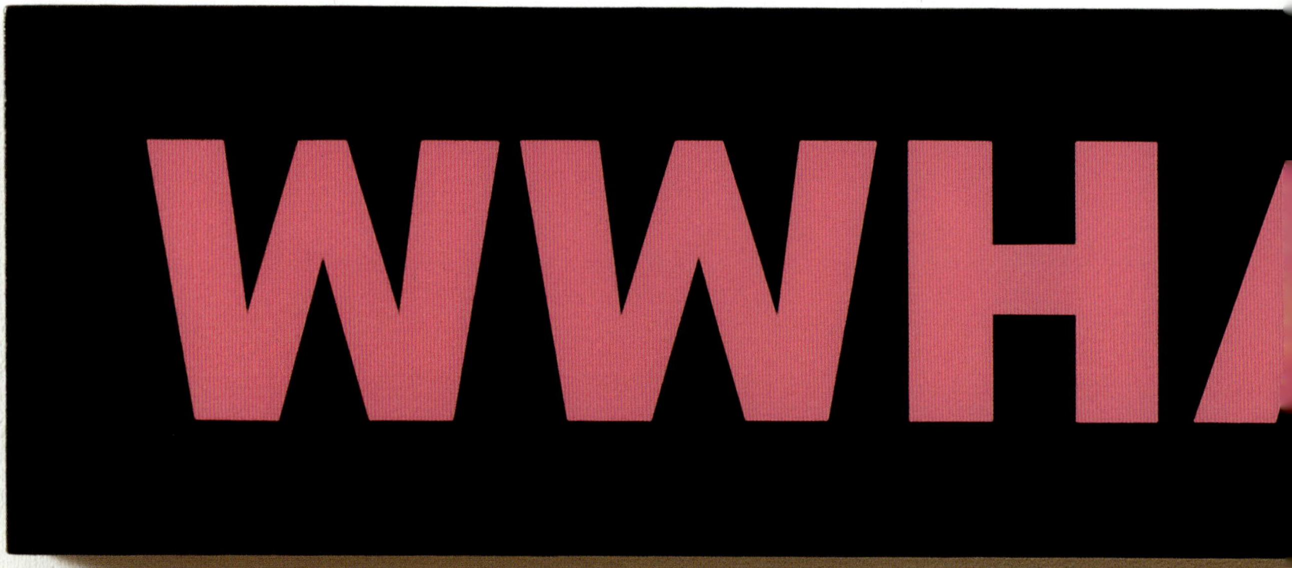

WWH

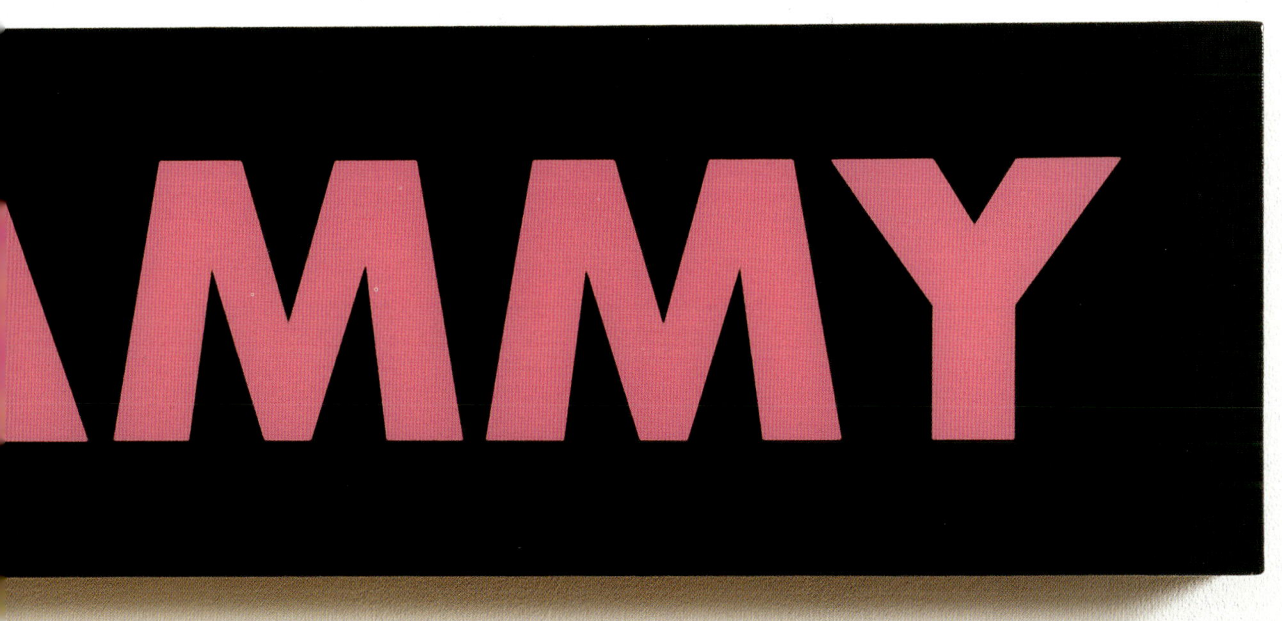
AMMY

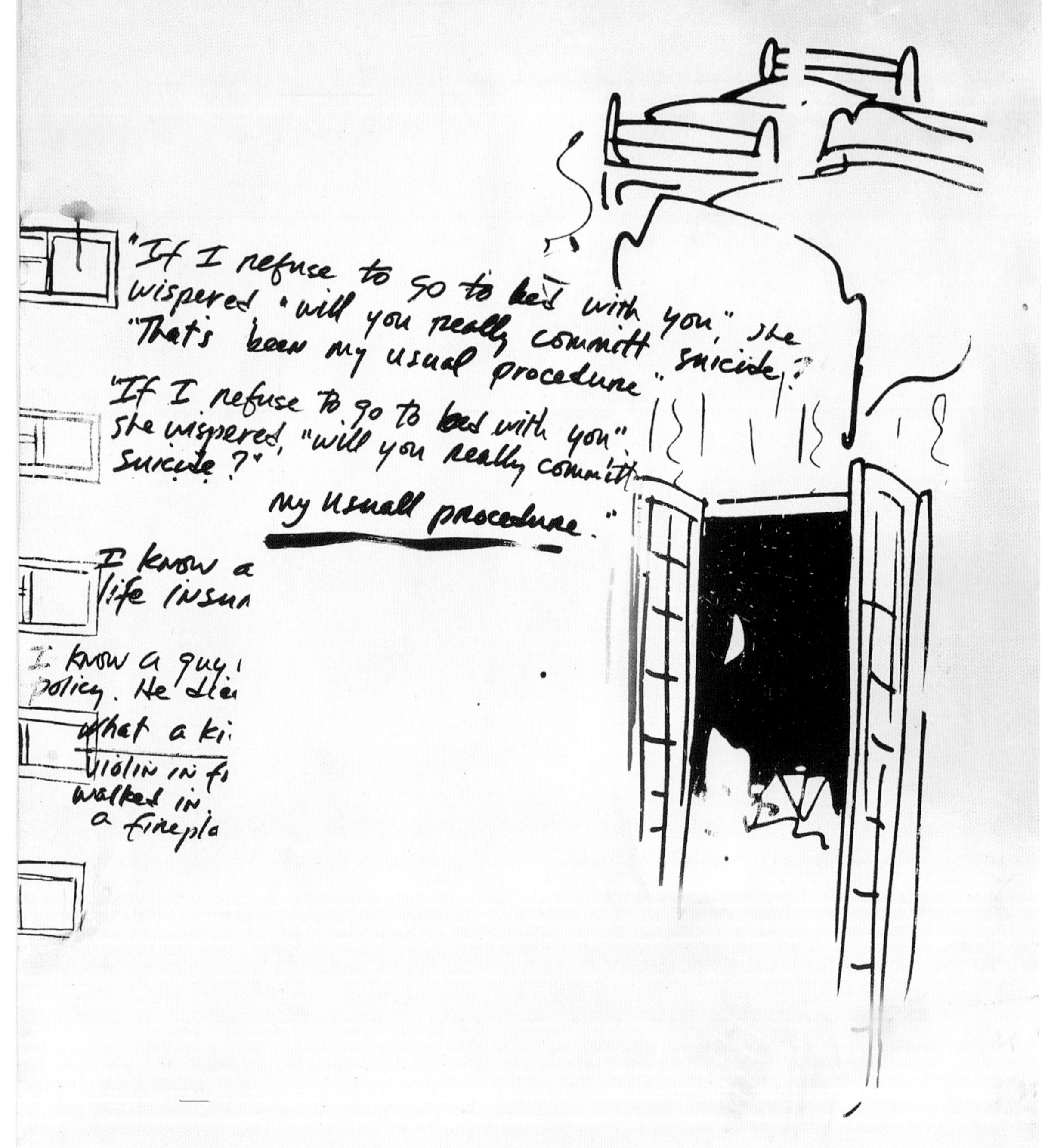

A man walked into a doctor's office to get a check-up. After the examination the Doctor said, "I've got good news and I've got bad news. The bad news is that your going to die in a year and there's nothing that can be done about it. The good news is that I'm having an affair with my new secretary.

GOOD NEWS AND BAD NEWS: A man walked into a doctor's office to get a check-up. After the examinadeeper reflections on various facets of the human condition that move far beyond the "one-liner." Given the ruthlessly immediate and complex changes that shape our reality, there is an increasing need for comedic expressions created not only for entertainment but to refocus attention onto the unsettling contingencies and increased complexities of contemporary existence.

Endnotes

1. Charles Baudelaire, "On the Essence of Laughter" (1855), in *The Painter of Modern Life and Other Essays*, translated and edited by Jonathan Mayne, London: Phaidon Press, 1995, 147–65.

2. Arthur Koestler, *Insight and Outlook. An inquiry into the common foundations of science, art, and social ethics*, New York: Macmillan, 1949, 56.

3. Steve Martin, *Comedy Is Not Pretty*, Warner Brothers Records, 1979, spoken word audio recording.

4. For a thorough and engaging history of the Situationists, see Greil Marcus's *Lipstick Traces: A Secret History of the Twentieth Century*, Cambridge, MA: Harvard University Press, 1990.

5. Henri Bergson, *Laughter: An Essay on the Meaning of the Comic* (1900), translated by Cloudesley Brereton and Fred Rothwell, accessed online at Project Gutenberg Editions, www.gutenberg.net/etext03/laemc10.txt.

6. James Thurber. Transcript of Ed Murrow's televison show Small World, CBS-TV (March 25, 1959). New York Post.

7. Woody Allen, from "My Philosophy," in *Getting Even*, New York: Vintage Books, 1978, 25.

8. Peter Land, quoted in Jan Estep, "Why Is Failure So Funny? Or A Funny Thing Happened on the Way to the Gallery: Buster Keaton and Peter Land," *New Art Examiner*, October 1998, 24.

Richard Prince

***Good News, Bad News*, 1989**
Acrylic and silkscreen on canvas
71 x 48 inches (180.3 x 121.9 cm)
Collection Museum of Contemporary Art, Chicago,
Gerald S. Elliott Collection

Laura Nova

On the Spot, 2001
Interactive installation with stage set, video, and sound
Approximately 120 x 204 x 84 inches
(304.8 x 518.2 x 213.4 cm)
Collection of the artist

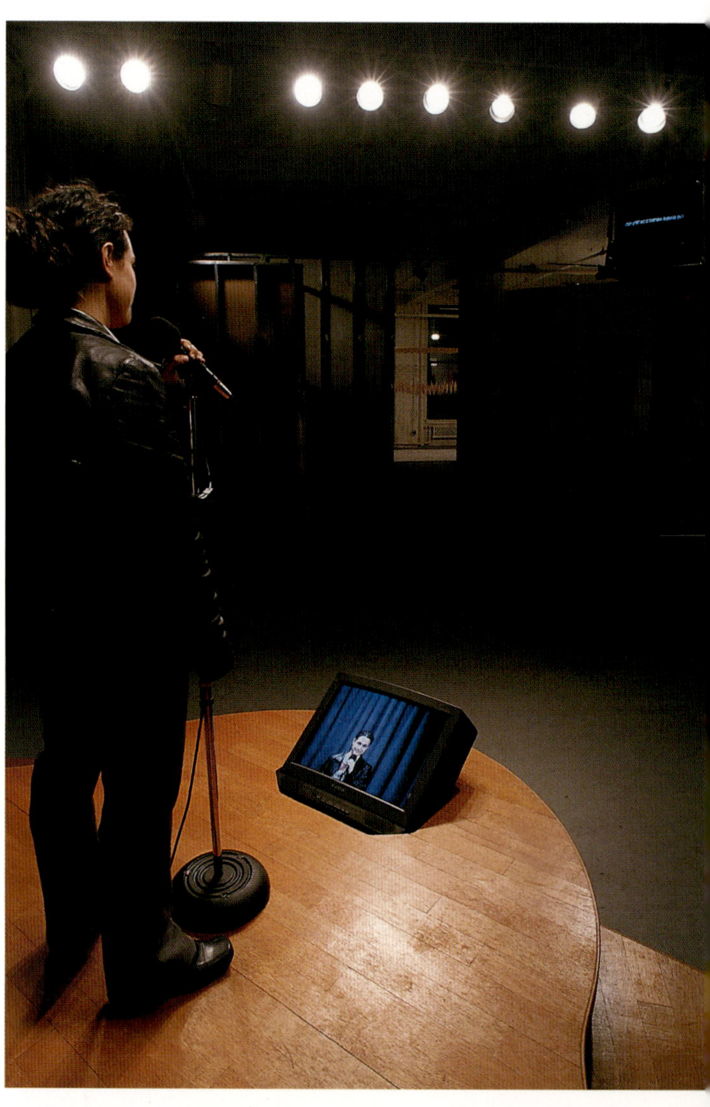

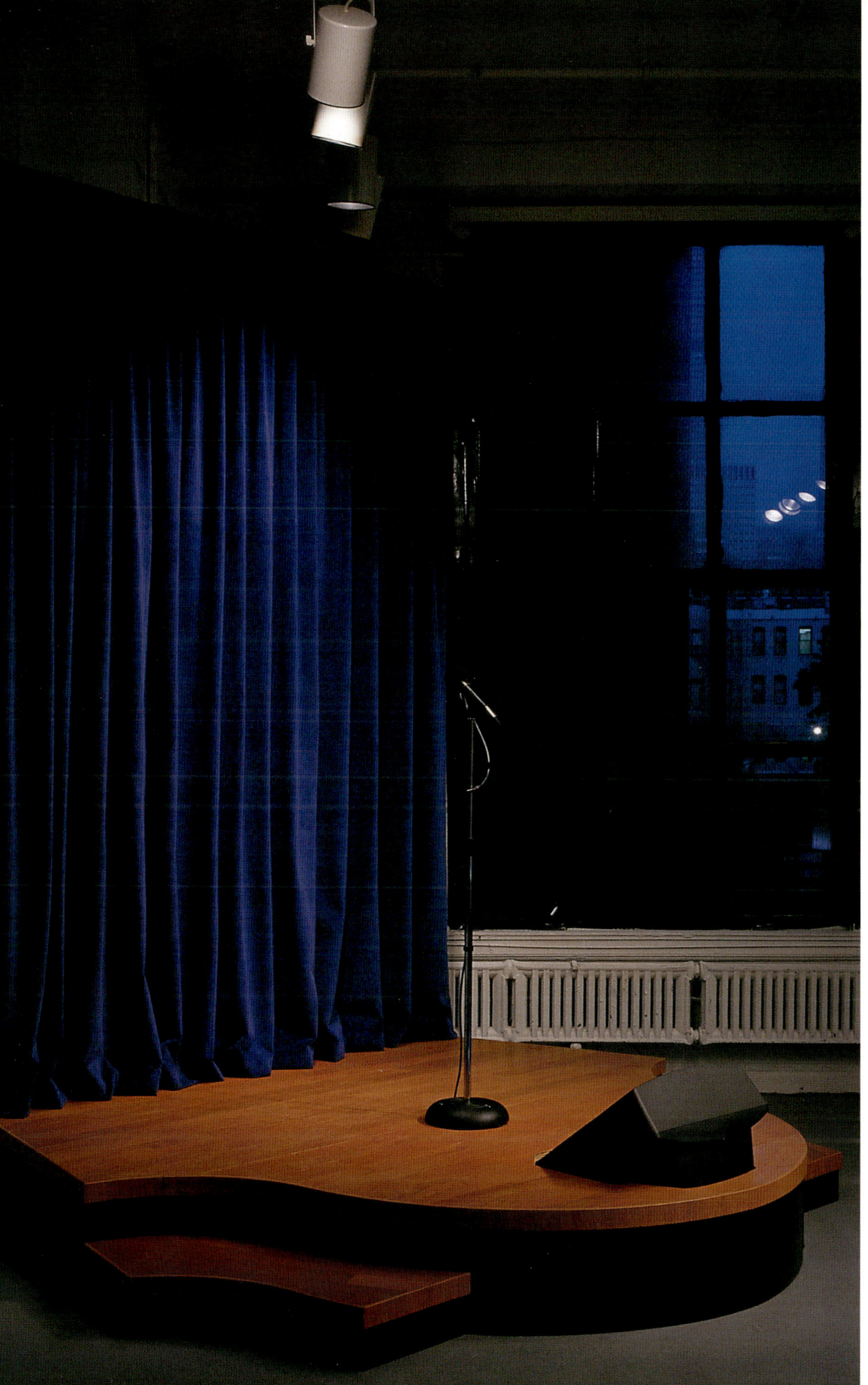

The First Six Moments from Twelve Moments in the Life of the Artist

David Sedaris

sunsets—and then, once he'd filled the basement walls with his efforts he stopped painting as mysteriously as he'd begun. It seemed to me that if my father could be an artist, anyone could. Snatching up his palette and brushes, I retreated to my bedroom, where, at the age of fourteen, I began my long and disgraceful blue period.

Two: When painting proved too difficult, I turned to tracing comic-book characters onto onionskin typing paper, telling myself that I would have come up with Mr. Natural on my own had I been born a few years earlier. The main thing was to stay focused and provide myself with realistic goals. Unlike my father, who blindly churned out one canvas after another, I had real ideas about the artistic life. Seated at my desk, my beret as tight as an acorn's cap, I projected myself into the world represented in the art books I'd borrowed from the public library. Leafing past the paintings, I would admire the photographs of the artists seated in their garrets, dressed in tattered smocks and frowning in the direction of their beefy nude models. To spend your days in the company of naked men—that was the life for me. "Turn a bit to the left, Jean-Claude. I long to capture the playful quality of your buttocks."

I envisioned the finicky curators coming to my door and begging me to hold another show at the Louvre or the Metropolitan. After a lunch of white wine and tongue-size cutlets, we would retire to the gentlemen's lounge and talk about money. I could clearly see the results of my labor the long satin scarves and magazine covers were very real to me. What I couldn't begin to imagine was the artwork itself. The only crimp in my plan was that I seemed to have no talent whatsoever. This was made clear when I signed up for art classes in high school. Asked to render a bowl of grapes, I would turn in what resembled a pile of stones hovering above a whitewall tire. My sister's paintings were prominently displayed on the walls of the classroom, and the teacher invoked her name whenever discussing perspective or color. She was included in all the city- and countywide shows and never mentioned the blue ribbons scotch-taped to her entries. Had she been a braggart, it would have been much easier to hate her. As it was, I had to wrestle daily with both my inadequacy and my uncontrollable jealousy. I didn't want to kill her, but hoped someone else might do the job for me.

Three: Away from home and the inevitable comparisons with Gretchen I enrolled as an art major at a college known mainly for its animal-husbandry program. The night before my first life-drawing class, I lay awake worrying that I might get physically excited by the nude models. Here would be this person, hopefully a strapping animal-husbandry major displaying his tanned and muscled body before an audience of students who, with the exception of me, would see him as nothing but an armature of skin and bones. Would the teacher take note of my bulging eyes or comment on the thin strand of saliva hanging like fishing wire from the corner of my mouth? Could I skip the difficult hands and feet and just concentrate on the parts that interested me, or would I be forced to sketch the entire figure?

My fears were genuine but misplaced. Yes, the model was beefy and masculine, but she was also a woman. Staring too hard was never an issue, as I was too busy trying to copy my neighbor's drawings. The teacher made his rounds from easel to easel, and I monitored his progress with growing panic. Maybe he didn't know my sister, but there were still plenty of other talented students to compare me with.

Frustrated with drawing, I switched to the printmaking department, where I overturned great buckets of ink. After trying my hand at sculpture, I attempted pottery. During class critiques the teacher would lift my latest project from the table and I'd watch her arm muscles strain and tighten against the weight. With their thick, clumsy bases, my mugs weighed in at close to five pounds each. The color was muddy and the lips rough and uninviting. I gave my mother a matching set for Christmas, and she accepted them as graciously as possible, announcing that they would make the perfect pet bowls. The mugs were set on the kitchen floor and remained there until the cat chipped a tooth and went on a hunger strike.

Four: I transferred to another college and started the whole humiliating process all over again. After switching from lithography to clay modeling, I stopped attending classes altogether, preferring to concentrate on what my roommate and I referred to as the "Bong Studies Program." A new set of owlish glasses made pinpoints of my red-rimmed eyes, and I fell in with a crowd of lazy filmmakers who talked big but wound up spending their production allowances on gummy bricks of hash. In their company I attended grainy black-and-white movies in which ponderous, turtlenecked men slogged the stony beaches, cursing the gulls for their ability to fly. The camera would cut to a field of ragged crows and then to a freckle-faced woman who sat in a sunbeam examining her knuckles. It was all I could do to stay awake until the movie ended and I could file out of the theater behind the melancholy ticketholders, who bore a remarkable resemblance to the pale worrywarts I'd seen flickering up on the screen. True art was based upon despair, and the important thing was to make yourself and those around you as miserable as possible. Maybe I couldn't paint or sculpt, but I could work a mood better than anyone I knew. Unfortunately, the school had no accredited sulking program and I dropped out, more despondent than ever.

Five: My sister Gretchen was leaving for the Rhode Island School of Design just as I was settling back into Raleigh. After a few months in my parents' basement, I took an apartment near the state university, where I discovered both crystal methamphetamine and conceptual art. Either one of these things is dangerous, but in combination they have the potential to destroy entire civilizations. The moment I took my first burning snootful, I understood that this was the drug for me. Speed eliminates all doubt. Am I smart enough? Will people like me? Do I really look all right in this plastic jumpsuit?

These are questions for insecure potheads. A speed enthusiast knows that everything he says or does is brilliant. The upswing is that, having eliminated the need for both eating and sleeping, you have a full twenty-four hours a day to spread your charm and talent.

"For God's sake," my father would say, "it's two o'clock in the morning. What are you calling for?"

I was calling because the rest of my friends had taken to unplugging their phones after ten P.M. These were people I'd known in high school, and it disappointed me to see how little we now had in common. They were still talking about pen-and-ink portraits and couldn't understand my desire to drag a heavy cash register through the forest. I hadn't actually *done* it, but it sounded like a good idea to me. These people were all stuck in the past, setting up their booths at the art fair and thinking themselves successful because they'd sold a silk screen of a footprint in the sand. It was sad in a way. Here they were, struggling to make art, while without the least bit of effort, I was *living* art. My socks balled up on the hardwood floor made a greater statement than any of their hokey claptrap with the carefully matted frames and big curly signatures in the lower left-hand corners. Didn't they read any of the magazines? The new breed of artist wanted nothing to do with my sister's idea of beauty. Here were people who made a living pitching tents or lying in a fetal position before our national monuments. One fellow had made a name for himself by allowing a friend to shoot him in the shoulder. This was the art world I'd been dreaming of, where God-given talent was considered an unfair advantage and a cold-blooded stare merited more praise than the ability to render human flesh. Everything around me was art, from the stains in my bathtub to the razor blade and short length of drinking straw I used to cut and ingest my speed. I was back in the world with a clear head and a keen vision of just how talented I really was.

"Let me put your mother on," my father would say. "She's had a few drinks, so maybe she can understand whatever the hell it is you're talking about."

Six: I bought my drugs from a jittery, bug-eyed typesetter whose brittle prematurely white hair was permed in such a way that I couldn't look at her without thinking of a late-season dandelion. Selling me the drugs was no problem, but listening to my increasingly manic thoughts and opinions was far too much for one person to take on a daily basis.

"I'm thinking of parceling off portions of my brain," I once told her. "I'm not talking about having anything surgically removed. I'd just like to divide it into lots and lease it out so that people could say, 'I've got a house in Raleigh, a cottage in Myrtle Beach, and a little hideaway inside a visionary's head.' "

Her bored expression suggested the questionable value of my mental real estate. Speed heats the brain to a full boil, leaving the mouth to function as a fulminating exhaust pipe. I talked until my tongue bled, my jaw gave out, and my throat swelled up in protest.

Hoping to get me off her back, my dealer introduced me to half a dozen hyperactive brainiacs who shared my taste for amphetamines and love of the word *manifesto*. Here, finally, was my group. The first meeting was tense, but I broke the ice by laying out a few lines of crystal and commenting on my host's refreshing lack of furniture. His living room contained nothing but an enormous nest made of human hair. It seemed that he drove twice a week to all the local beauty parlors and barbershops collecting their sweepings and arranging them, strand by strand, as carefully as a wren.

"I've been building this nest for, oh, about six months now," he said. "Go ahead, have a seat."

Other group members stored their bodily fluids in babyfood jars or wrote cryptic messages on packaged skirt steaks. Their artworks were known as "pieces," a phrase I enthusiastically embraced. "Nice piece," I'd say. In my eagerness to please, I accidentally complimented chipped baseboards and sacks of laundry waiting to be taken to the cleaners. Anything might be a piece if you looked at it hard enough. High on crystal, the gang and I would tool down the beltway, admiring the traffic cones and bright yellow speed bumps. The art world was our conceptual oyster, and we ate it raw.

Inspired by my friends, I undertook a few pieces of my own. My first project was a series of wooden vegetable crates I meticulously filled with my garbage. Seeing as how I no longer ate anything, there were no rotting food scraps to worry about, just cigarette butts, aspirin tins, wads of undernourished hair, and bloody Kleenex. Because these were pieces, I carefully recorded each entry using an ink I'd made from the crushed bodies of ticks and mosquitoes.

2:17 A.M.: Four toenail clippings.

3:48 A.M.: Eyelash discovered beside sink. Moth.

Once the first two crates were completed, I carried them down to the art museum for consideration in their upcoming juried biennial. When the notice arrived that my work had been accepted, I foolishly phoned my friends with the news. Their proposals to set fire to the grand staircase or sculpt the governor's head out of human feces had all been rejected

This officially confirmed their outsider status and made me an enemy of the avant-garde. At the next group meeting it was suggested that the museum had accepted my work only because it was decorative and easy to swallow. My friends could have gotten in had they compromised themselves, but unlike me, some people had integrity.

Plans were made for an alternative exhibit, and I wound up attending the museum opening in the company of my mother and my drug dealer, who by this time had lost so much hair and weight that, in her earth-tone sheath, she resembled a cocktail onion speared on a toothpick. The two of them made quite a pair, hogging the wet bar and loudly sharing their uninformed opinions with anyone within earshot. There was a little jazz combo playing in the corner, and the waiters circulated with trays of jumbo shrimp and stuffed mushrooms. I observed the crowd gathered around my crates, wanting to overhear their comments but feeling a deeper need to keep tabs on my mother. I looked over at one point and caught her drunkenly clutching the arm of the curator, shouting, “I just passed a lady in the bathroom and told her, ‘Honey, why flush it? Carry it into the next room and they’ll put it on a goddamn pedestal.’ “

exhibition checklist

Note: height precedes width precedes depth; all dimensions unframed unless otherwise specified

Stephanie Brooks

Born 1970, Hammond, Indiana
Resides Chicago, Illinois

Untitled from the *Politeness Strategy* series, 2002
Enamel on etched zinc
5 x 7 inches (12.7 x 17.8 cm)
Collection of Cleve E. Carney
page 53

Untitled from the *Politeness Strategy* series, 2002
Enamel on etched zinc
5 x 7 inches (12.7 x 17.8 cm)
Collection of Cleve E. Carney
page 72

Untitled from the *Politeness Strategy* series, 2002
Enamel on etched zinc
5 x 7 inches (12.7 x 17.8 cm)
Collection of Cleve E. Carney

Michael Elmgreen and Ingar Dragset

Elmgreen born 1961, Copenhagen, Denmark
Dragset born 1969, Trondheim, Norway
Both reside in Berlin, Germany

Powerless Structures (*Safe*), 2000
Stainless steel, combination lock, canvas, and stretcher
35½ x 35½ x 2 inches (90.2 x 90.2 x 5.1 cm)
Collection of Burt Minkoff, Lake Worth, Florida
page 23

Tom Friedman

Born 1965, St. Louis, Missouri
Resides Northampton, Massachusetts

Untitled, 1994
Black and white photograph
35 x 25 inches (88.9 x 63.5 cm)
Private collection;
courtesy Neal Meltzer Fine Art, Inc.

Untitled, 1996
Cibachrome print
3 x 6⅛ inches (7.6 x 15.6 cm)
Private collection;
courtesy Neal Meltzer Fine Art, Inc.
page 38

Luis Gispert

Born 1972, Jersey City, New Jersey
Resides Brooklyn, New York

Block Watching, 2002-03
Single-channel video with sound
1 minute, 57 seconds
Collection of the artist;
courtesy Zach Feuer Gallery (LFL), New York
pages 14-15

Felix Gmelin

Born 1962, Heidelberg, Germany
Resides Stockholm, Sweden

I Love You Tushee Love Buns (After Roy Lichtenstein [1962] and Reginald Walker [1993]), 1994
Oil on polyester
39 x 33½ inches framed (100 x 85 cm)
Collection of the artist;
courtesy Milliken, Stockholm and maccarone, inc., New York
page 24

Rodney Graham

Born 1949, Vancouver, Canada
Resides Vancouver, Canada

Vexation Island, 1997
Single-channel video with sound from 35mm film transferred to laser disc
9 minutes, continuous loop
Collection of the artist;
courtesy Donald Young Gallery, Chicago
pages 34-35

Christian Jankowski

Born 1968, Göttingen, Germany
Resides New York, New York

The Hunt, 1992
Single-channel video with sound
1 minute, 11 seconds
Collection of the artist;
courtesy maccarone, inc., New York and Klosterfelde, Berlin
pages 10-11

Flock, 2002
Single-channel video with sound
12 minutes, 15 seconds
Collection of the artist;
courtesy maccarone, inc., New York and Klosterfelde, Berlin

Martin Kersels

Born 1960, Los Angeles, California
Resides Los Angeles, California

Tossing a Friend (Melinda) (1, 2, and 3), 1996
Three Cibachrome prints
Each: 34½ x 46½ inches framed (87.6 x 118.1 cm)
Collection of Burt Aaron, Detroit, Michigan
page 40

Alexej Koschkarow

Born 1972, Minsk, Bela Russia.
Resides Düsseldorf, Germany

Tortenschlacht (Pie Fight), 2003
Single-channel video with sound
13 minutes
Collection of the artist;
courtesy Jablonka Lühn, Cologne
pages 36-37

Peter Land

Born 1966, Aarhus, Denmark
Resides Copenhagen, Denmark

Pink Space, 1995
Single-channel video with sound
17 minutes, 35 seconds
Collection of the artist;
courtesy Galleri Nicolai Wallner, Copenhagen
page 33

Cary Leibowitz

Born 1963, New York, New York
Resides New York, New York

Self Esteem 100 Dollars, Reduced to 5 Cents, 1995
Latex house paint on wood
30 x 17½ inches (76.2 x 44.5 cm)
Collection of Scott Lorinsky;
courtesy Andrew Kreps Gallery, New York
page 30

Please Check One, 1999
Latex house paint on wood
32 x 18½ inches (81.3 x 47 cm)
Collection of Burt Aaron, Detroit, Michigan

Gain! Wait! Now!, 2001
Garbage cans and umbrella stands
Approximately 76 x 43 x 43 inches
(193 x 109.2 x 109.2 cm)
Courtesy of the artist and
Andrew Kreps Gallery, New York

Kelly Mark

Born 1967, Welland, Ontario
Resides Toronto, Ontario

I really should...1,000, 2002
Audio CD with headphones
58 minutes
Courtesy Wynick/Tuck Gallery, Toronto and Tracey Lawrence Gallery, Toronto

Reuben, 2003
Single-channel video
15 minutes, 30 seconds
Courtesy Wynick/Tuck Gallery, Toronto and Tracey Lawrence Gallery, Toronto
page 52

Dave Muller

Born 1964, San Francisco, California
Resides Los Angeles, California

He could sell ice to..., 2000
Acrylic and aluminum paint on paper
Two parts, 20 x 64 inches overall
(50.8 x 162.6 cm)
Private collection, New York
page 18

Laura Nova

Born 1973, West Hartford, Connecticut
Resides New York, New York

On the Spot, 2001
Interactive installation with stage set, video, and sound
Approximately 120 x 204 x 84 inches
(304.8 x 518.2 x 213.4 cm)
Collection of the artist
pages 58-59

William Pope.L

Born 1955, Newark, New Jersey
Resides Lewiston, Maine

Foraging #1 (The Funk) from the series *Black Domestic*, 1995-98
Cibachrome print
52 x 40 inches, framed (132.1 x 101.6 cm)
Courtesy of the artist and Projectile Gallery

Foraging #2 (Animal Husbandry) from the series *Black Domestic*, 1995-98
Cibachrome print
52 x 40 inches, framed (132.1 x 101.6 cm)
Courtesy of the artist and Projectile Gallery

Foraging #3 (The Air Itself) from the series *Black Domestic*, 1995-98
Cibachrome print
52 x 40 inches, framed (132.1 x 101.6 cm)
Courtesy of the artist and Projectile Gallery
page 26

Richard Prince

Born 1949, Panama Canal Zone
Resides New York state

Good News, Bad News, 1989
Acrylic and silkscreen on canvas
71 x 48 inches (180.3 x 121.9 cm)
Collection Museum of Contemporary Art, Chicago, Gerald S. Elliott Collection
page 56

David Robbins

Born 1957, Whitefish Bay, Wisconsin
Resides Milwaukee, Wisconsin

Self-Parody, 1993
Gelatin silver prints
Eighteen parts overall. Seventeen parts,
each 10 x 8 inches (25.4 x 20.3 cm);
one part, 8 x 10 inches (20.3 x 25.4 cm)
Collection Museum of Contemporary Art, Chicago, gift of James Mark Pedersen
pages 48-49

Kay Rosen

Born 1943, Corpus Christi, Texas
Resides Gary, Indiana

Double Whammy, 1993
Enamel sign paint on canvas
10 x 50 inches (25.4 x 127 cm)
Collection of Peter Norton, Santa Monica
pages 54-55

Aunt Bea, 1994
Enamel sign paint on canvas
20 x 24 inches (50.8 x 61 cm)
Collection of the artist

Erika Rothenberg

Born 1950, New York, New York
Resides Los Angeles, California

Another Century of Progress, 1999-2000
Aluminum and acrylic signboard, plastic letters
36 x 24 x 1¾ inches (91.4 x 61 x 4.4 cm)
Collection of the artist;
courtesy Zolla/Lieberman Gallery, Chicago
page 13

Dana Schutz

Born 1976, Livonia, Michigan
Resides New York, New York

Sneeze 2, 2001
Oil on canvas
20 x 19 inches (50.8 x 48.2 cm)
Private collection

Sneeze (Blonde Woman), 2001
Oil on canvas
19 x 19 inches (48.2 x 48.2 cm)
Collection of Brooke and Erik Parker, New York
page 42

Lawrence Seward

Born 1966, Honolulu, Hawaii
Resides New York, New York

Untitled, 2000
Rubber, metal, plaster, and acrylic paint
2½ x 17 x 25½ inches (6.4 x 43.2 x 64.8 cm)
Collection of Erin H. McKinnon, New York
page 45

David Shrigley

Born 1968, Macclesfield, England
Resides Glasgow, Scotland

Untitled (The Hunter), 1997
Ink on paper
8¼ x 5¾ inches (21 x 14.5 cm)
Collection of Stephanie Theodore, New York

Untitled (Special Pincer Tool), 1997
Ink on paper
6 x 4 inches (15 x 10 cm)
Collection of Stephanie Theodore, New York

Untitled (That Bloke We Met on Holiday), 1997
Ink on paper
6 x 4 inches (15 x 10 cm)
Collection of Stephanie Theodore, New York

Untitled (Numbers of the Beast), 1998
Ink on paper
9½ x 10¼ inches (24 x 26 cm)
Collection of Stephanie Theodore, New York

Untitled (An Honest Voice in a World of Lies), 1998
Ink on paper
6 x 4 inches (15 x 10 cm)
Collection of Stephanie Theodore, New York

Untitled (Don't Bother to Try to Kill the Flies), 1998
Ink on paper
9⅝ x 10¼ inches (24.5 x 26 cm)
Collection of Richard Lappin,
Brooklyn, New York

Untitled (The Foam Block), 1998
Ink on paper
6 x 4 inches (15 x 10 cm)
Collection of Richard Lappin,
Brooklyn, New York

Untitled (Fools Rush In), 1998
Ink on paper
6 x 4 inches (15 x 10 cm)
Collection of Richard Lappin,
Brooklyn, New York

Untitled (Notice), 1998
Chromogenic print
9⅞ x 9⅞ inches (25 x 25 cm)
Collection of Richard Lappin,
Brooklyn, New York
pages 20-21

Untitled (Drink Me), 1998
Chromogenic print
9⅞ x 9⅞ inches (25 x 25 cm)
Collection of Richard Lappin,
Brooklyn, New York

Untitled (Sunday Adventure Club), 1998
Chromogenic print
9⅞ x 9⅞ inches (25 x 25 cm)
Collection of Richard Lappin,
Brooklyn, New York

Untitled (Go to Hell, You'll Probably Enjoy It), 1999
Ink on paper
9½ x 8¼ inches (24 x 21 cm)
Collection of Stephanie Theodore, New York

Untitled (Don't Worry, Your World Isn't Falling Apart), 2000
Ink on paper
13 x 11¾ inches (33 x 30 cm)
Collection of Stephanie Theodore, New York

Untitled (From Now On I Will Do Exactly As I Am Told), 2000
Ink and tempera on paper
15¾ x 14 inches (40 x 35.5 cm)
Collection of Stephanie Theodore, New York

Untitled (The Grizzly Event), 2002
Mixed media on paper
15¼ x 12 inches (40 x 30.5 cm)
Collection of Richard Lappin,
Brooklyn, New York

Bob and Roberta Smith

Born 1964, London, United Kingdom
Resides London, United Kingdom

Make Your Own Damn Art, 2001
Acrylic on cotton
73 x 70 inches (185.4 x 177.8 cm)
Collection of the artist;
courtesy Pierogi Gallery, Brooklyn, New York
page 17

Artists Ruin it For Everyone, 2001
Acrylic on cotton
75 x 69 inches (190.5 x 175.3 cm)
Collection of the artist;
courtesy Pierogi Gallery, Brooklyn, New York

Michael Smith

Born 1951, Chicago, Illinois
Resides Brooklyn, New York

OYMA (Outstanding Young Men of America), 1996
Single-channel video with sound
9 minutes, 23 seconds
Courtesy Electronic Arts Intermix, New York
page 32

Susan Smith-Pinelo

Born 1969, Duxbury, Massachusetts
Resides Washington, D.C.

Sometimes, 2001
Single-channel video with sound
4 minutes, 58 seconds
Courtesy of Fusebox, Washington, D.C.
pages 28-29

Tony Tasset

Born 1960, Cincinnati, Ohio
Resides Oak Park, Illinois

I Peed in My Pants, 1994
Cibachrome print
83¼ x 38¼ inches framed (211.5 x 97.2 cm)
Collection of Refco Group, Ltd.
page 41

John Waters

Born 1946, Baltimore, Maryland
Resides Baltimore, Maryland

In My Mind, 1998
Cibachrome print
16 x 20 inches (40.6 x 50.8 cm)
Collection of the artist and Marianne Boesky Gallery, New York

Visit Marfa, 2003
Offset print
30 x 22 inches (76.2 x 55.9 cm)
Collection of the artist and Marianne Boesky Gallery, New York
page 51

Olav Westphalen

Born 1963, Hamburg, Germany
Resides New York, New York

Snowman, 2002-03
Acrylic and ink on paper
30 x 23 inches framed (76.2 x 58.4 cm)
Collection of the artist;
courtesy maccarone, inc., New York
page 19

Banana Peel, 2002-03
Acrylic and ink on paper
36 x 26 inches framed (91.4 x 66 cm)
Collection of the artist;
courtesy maccarone, inc., New York

I Love Holland, 2002-03
Acrylic and ink on paper
31 x 23 inches framed (78.7 x 58.4 cm)
Collection of the artist;
courtesy maccarone, inc., New York

Useful Props for Mimes with Political Tendencies, 2002-03
Acrylic and ink on paper
20 x 16 inches framed (50.8 x 40.6 cm)
Collection of the artist;
courtesy maccarone, inc., New York

The Big Book of Book-Knowledge, 2002-03
Acrylic and ink on paper
36 x 26 inches framed (91.4 x 66 cm)
Collection of the artist;
courtesy maccarone, inc., New York

German Guilt, 2002-03
Acrylic and ink on paper
11 x 9 inches framed (27.9 x 22.9 cm)
Collection of the artist;
courtesy maccarone, inc., New York

Erwin Wurm
Born 1954, Mur, Austria
Resides Vienna, Austria

Looking for a Bomb 2 from the series *Instructions on How to Be Politically Incorrect*, 2003
Cibachrome print mounted on aluminum under Plexiglas
50 x 73 inches (126 x 184 cm)
Collection of the artist;
courtesy Jack Hanley Gallery, San Francisco

Looking for a Bomb 3 from the series *Instructions on How to Be Politically Incorrect*, 2003
Cibachrome print mounted on aluminum under Plexiglas
50 x 73 inches (126 x 184 cm)
Collection of the artist;
courtesy Jack Hanley Gallery, San Francisco
pages 46-47

iCI board of trustees

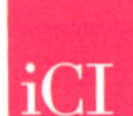

Celebrating its 30th anniversary in 2005, iCI is a dynamic non-profit organization committed to enhancing the understanding and appreciation of contemporary art through its innovative traveling exhibitions and publications. iCI brings challenging artworks to a wide range of museums, giving diverse audiences in the United States and abroad the opportunity to experience new art.

lenders to the exhibition

Burt Aaron
Marianne Boesky Gallery, New York
Cleve E. Carney
Electronic Arts Intermix (EAI), New York
Zach Feuer Gallery (LFL), New York
Fusebox, Washington, D.C.
Luis Gispert
Felix Gmelin
Rodney Graham
Jack Hanley Gallery, San Francisco
Jablonka Lühn, Cologne
Christian Jankowski
Alexej Koschkarow
Andrew Kreps Gallery, New York
Peter Land
Richard Lappin
Tracey Lawrence Gallery, Toronto
Cary Leibowitz
Scott Lorinsky
maccarone, inc., New York
Erin H. McKinnon
Neal Meltzer Fine Art, Inc.
Milliken, Stockholm
Burt Minkoff
Museum of Contemporary Art, Chicago
Peter Norton
Laura Nova
Brooke and Erik Parker
Pierogi Gallery, Brooklyn, New York
William Pope.L
Projectile Gallery, New York
Refco Group, Ltd., Chicago
Kay Rosen
Erika Rothenberg
Bob and Roberta Smith
Stephanie Theodore
Galleri Nicolai Wallner, Copenhagen
John Waters
Olav Westphalen
Erwin Wurm
Wynick/Tuck Gallery, Toronto
Donald Young Gallery, Chicago
Zolla/Lieberman Gallery, Chicago

photo credits: Tim Thayer, front cover, p. 40; maccarone, inc., New York, pp. 10-11, 19; Erika Rothenberg, p. 13; Luis Gispert, pp. 14-15; Pierogi Gallery, Brooklyn, p. 17; Blum & Poe, Los Angeles, Photo: Joshua White, p. 18; David Shrigley, pp. 20-21; Tanya Bonakdar Gallery, New York, p. 23; Milliken, Stockholm, p. 24; William Pope.L, p. 26; Fusebox, Washington, D.C., pp. 28-29; Photo: Jeffrey Sturges, pp. 30, 38, 45; Electronic Arts Intermix (EAI), New York, p. 32; Galleri Nicolai Wallner, Copenhagen, p. 33; Donald Young Gallery, Chicago, pp. 34-35; Jablonka Lühn, Cologne, pp. 36-37; Refco Collection, Photo: Michael Tropea, Chicago, p. 41; Zach Feuer Gallery (LFL), New York, p. 42; Erwin Wurm, pp. 46-47; David Robbins, pp. 48-49; Marianne Boesky Gallery, New York, p. 51; Kelly Mark, p. 52; Stephanie Brooks, pp. 53, 72; Kay Rosen, Photo: Peter Muscato; pp. 54-55; © Museum of Contemporary Art, Chicago, p. 56; Laura Nova, pp. 58-59.

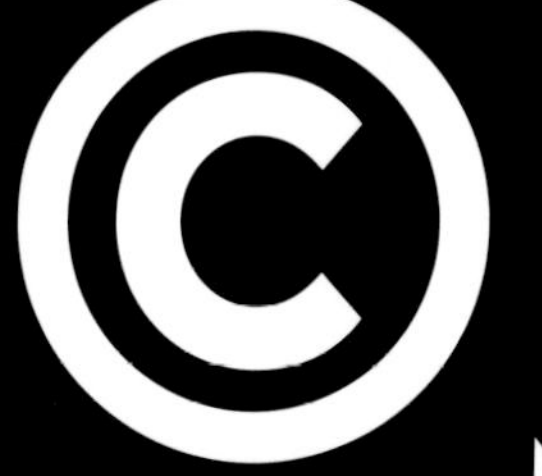

799 Broadway, Suite 205
New York, NY 10003
Tel: 212-254-8200 Fax: 212-477-4781
www.ici-exhibitions.org

Library of Congress: 2005925940
ISBN: 0-916365-72-7
Editor: Deborah Drier
Design by mgmt. design
Printed by Transcontinental-Litho Acme, Montreal

You have a nice { day. / ass. / attitude.